G000300629

Mata Yogananda Mahasaya Dharma

Self~Realization
Through
Pure Meditation

You are all the fruits of the tree.

Self~Realization
Through
Pure Meditation

Mata Yogananda
Mahasaya Dharma

Daoseva Press

Second edition (revised & expanded) © 2005

First Published © 1994

© Self Realization Meditation Healing Centre 2005

1 3 5 7 9 8 6 4 2

Published by
Daoseva Press
Laurel Lane, Queen Camel,
Yeovil, Somerset, BA22 7NU, UK

The Self Realization Meditation Healing Centre was founded by
Mata Yogananda and Peter Sevananda and the Daoseva Press
is its publishing branch.

ISBN   0 9522734 8 9

British Library Cataloguing–in–Publication Data.
A catalogue record for this book is available from
the British Library.

Typeset in DellaRobbia 10/12 pt.

by Daoseva Press

Printed and bound in Great Britain by
J. H. Haynes & Co. Ltd, Sparkford, UK.

The
Self Realization Meditation
Healing Centre

Came into being by

THE DIVINE WILL OF GOD
founded by
Mata Yogananda Mahasaya Dharma
&
Peter Sevananda

and taken forward by
The Alpha–Omega Family
who are
the direct disciples of
Mata Yogananda Mahasaya Dharma

They who serve
with Love, Wisdom
and Knowledge

Mata Yogananda
Mahasaya Dharma
~ and her work in this
lifetime

Mata Yogananda Mahasaya
Dharma is the Founder and
Spiritual Head of the Self
Realization Meditation Healing
Centres, and the Alpha~Omega
family who live and work in the UK Mother Centre
and the Sister Centres worldwide.

For many Mata Yoganandaji needs no introduction.

From an early age Mataji asked that she may
experience and know all the conditions of life. This
she did, travelling through the trials of life ~ marriage,
business, child–rearing, illness and separation~ to the
feet of her Gurudeva, Paramahansa Yogananda.

Paramahansa Yogananda reawakened Mataji for
her spiritual work in this lifetime. Mataji was asked to
teach Pure Meditation, so that all those who wish to
may find Self–Realization in this lifetime. Mataji was
also asked to train souls in order to spread God's work
worldwide.

The Self Realization Meditation Healing Centre
was founded by Mataji so that all in need may imbibe
there and receive spiritual guidance and training from
those who have faced similar life challenges. The
Alpha-Omega family who live and work at the

Mother Centre with Mataji's blessing, aim to live a God~Centred life with unconditional love ~ showing that it can be done.

The Mother Centre's permanent home is in Somerset, England, and its work has expanded worldwide. Further, Mataji has founded Sister Centres overseas, to help spread the light to all those searching souls wherever they may be.

Mataji is a true Guru ~ her every thought, word and deed is to spread light and love. Mataji's wish is that this book brings you the spiritual truth and guidance that you seek on your journey.

Dedication

This book, called *Self~Realization Through Pure Meditation*, is dedicated to all Masters for their deep love and devotion in helping souls towards Self~God~Realization.

My Gurudeva Paramahansa Yoganandaji, who awakes, once more, the Christ~God within me.

The many souls including T.B., Aranti, Rydal, Chi San Lu and many other spiritual souls who are forever helping in any way that they can from their spiritual realms.

I give thanks to all those Loving Souls, who have given their time willingly to this book.

Only people separate themselves from life,
from other people and the Infinite;
by thinking they are better or worse,
wrong or right.

The OM

Transcendental state
Maya
Wakeful state
Dreamless state
Dream state

We are in the dream state of dreams and
unknowing of knowledge.

We are in a dreamless state in between our dreams
and waking up – "time to wake up".

We are in a wakeful state when we realize we need
to look at life and ourselves.

We are in a maya state when we see and have
knowledge within our **selves** that all
is maya in life – a dream – dream thoughts.

We are in the transcendental state when we look
in our third eye and know that there is
no separation in life.

We are all one.

ONE ENERGY
ONE LIFE
IN ALL OF CREATION –

We are all One

Because ignorance
is the root of all our troubles –

Explaining and spreading the truth
is above all charities.

Buddha

Contents

Illustrations

ॐ

Introduction

Mata Yogananda Mahasaya Dharma lives purely to bring the joy of Pure Meditation, the opportunity to work towards Self–Realization in this lifetime to all people who desire it. She is a shining example of how to live in this world, yet not be of its materialism, negativity or conditioning. Mataji does not urge withdrawal from the world but rather to be yourself, be of love and still play your part: so this book about Pure Meditation is for everyone who has ever wanted to find true peace and spirituality in every moment or action and thought it impossible or elusive.

Guruji grew up in England, as Rena Denton, wanting to experience all of life that she might learn and help others. And experience she certainly found – in a tough world where the ideals she loved brought hardships of many kinds, mixing with people of all classes, races and religions until it was time for her life's purpose to begin.

Then in answer to her deep longing, she met her Gurudeva, Paramahansa Yoganandaji, who lovingly awakened her spiritual knowledge, telling her she was to be a Guru, would be the spiritual head and founder of a Centre for Meditation, and of the Alpha–Omega family. 'Why me?' came quickly to Mataji's lips.

'Surely there must be others who would have complete faith right away and would not a man be better for the task you have in mind for me?' Paramahansaji answered 'a woman who would not harm a soul, and with an abundance of love was needed and that strong faith came from testing it... not from blind faith'.

And from that strong faith, well tested, from that experience, from that abundant unconditional love, embraced by a willing desire to serve all of life, came with the speed of spiritual rightness over material impossibility, the Self Realization Meditation Healing Centre.

The Mother Centre in Somerset is now spiritual home to many people, giving teaching in the ancient, yet modern art and science of Pure, depth Meditation. And whilst there are many taking this teaching into their lives, the greatest care is taken of each individual's needs, for in our growth, in our individuality, we have a precious difference, one from another.

Out of the depth of her wisdom, and from the pure simplicity of her teaching, Mataji gives us the opportunity to see ourselves. All we have to ask is, are we willing to lay aside heartache, conditioning and material entrapment in order to be at peace? Are we ready to change ourselves? Do we want progress?

If our answer is *yes,* however hesitantly, we can take another step forward out of conflict into joy. The teachings are about life today and are for everyone *of every religion* – no restrictions, no limitations, no conditions – just how to find yourself and be yourself.

Gurudeva teaches by example, knows human experience and suffering and gives practical common sense spiritual solutions to ease confusion and heartache. How often I have heard someone saying with heartfelt appreciation and wonder – 'I didn't know I could ask a Guru about personal matters – it didn't seem spiritual but somehow it just came out and her love has lifted me into a new way of looking at life. Now I can see that there is nothing spirituality cannot touch'.

Mataji has played many roles in this life: wife, mother, teacher, counsellor, healer, cook, dancer, photographer, physiotherapist, car mechanic, nurse and many more. But look beyond the limitations of each facet and seekers of truth will find that Mata Yoganandaji will be whoever and whatever is needed of her at that point in time. When a solicitor said it was impossible to complete the purchase of the Mother Centre and have Charitable status granted in so short a time, Mataji, from inner wisdom, was able to simply tell him how it was possible – and it happened. We have witnessed how builders, plumbers and gardeners, time and time again stood back from a problem, only to hear Mataji quietly saying 'Have you thought of… ?' And then work progressed rapidly!

To have the privilege of being in Mataji's physical presence is sheer joy to the spirit: to have the gift of knowing her spiritual presence wherever you are and whatever you are doing is a source of wonderment, love and abiding happiness. To feel the touch of her love upon your heart will enrich your life beyond compare.

Gurudeva is One and lights for us all the path to Oneness.

Christy Casley
Disciple

Read and assimilate
Assimilate and practice
Practice and Find...
Your True Self

Foreword

This is a book written to help all peoples who are in
need, or in search of something that will change their
life... will bring them peace, contentment, and a good
full life, not only for themselves but for others
around them.

I want to make this an easy book to read and assimilate.
So that interested peoples who read these words know
that without doubt,

This is the Time for Self–Realization

and knowing the God within.
It is not difficult. With desire and patience it can be so.

This is written from many years of experience with
knowledge of Meditation, of varying kinds. I hope that
in this book you will find the answer
that you are looking for.

So may we commune together for this short while,
while I write of the science and the joys of
Pure Meditation, of peace, love and happiness
that is our birthright.

My love goes out to each and every one of you.

Mata Yogananda

Gurus~Masters wish nothing
from you but to respect,
be truthful to them
and listen to their words of wisdom
~ so you will progress.

Truths are Born

When the lips are closed,
Then the heart begins to speak.
When the heart is silent, then the soul flares up,
bursting into flame,
and this illuminates the whole of life.

Hazrat Inayat Khan

Meditation is one of the oldest, and best sciences brought to man and woman, to help them find themselves and find that they can and do have love and happiness in this life time.

It was long before Jesus' time that the great Seers found out about the value of Meditation.

Feeling that there must be more than flesh and bone, they set out by rituals and going inwardly, deeply and silently, to find and to prove that we were more than mere mortals.

These Priests and Seers slowly, with years of devout patience and practice, found out about the great mysteries of life and death. That they, as humans, had great power, and could perform – what we now think of as – miracles.

All these findings were kept to themselves, and only passed on verbally, to those whom were found to be truly worthy to receive such great truths.

Many were turned away, and only a few were chosen.

The wise ones knew that if this knowledge got into the wrong hands, it would be misused and do harm.

When in that era, the peoples started to become more corrupt and less spiritual, there became few who wished for these truths.

The Priests were defiled and killed, and others fled, to die of old age, all of them taking their secret findings to the grave, to await another epoch, when somewhere in time, some soul would bring forth these findings again.

There are millennia of life times. We must be left to live all these eras, until it becomes time for the truths to be retold.

Master Seers are then reborn, and travel both in mind and body to different parts of the globe to speak of these *Truths,* hidden for so long.

Bearing in mind that all happenings of mind, body and spirit are stored in the ether... it just takes the re–birthing of Master Souls in the correct time and place, to make, the correct evolutionary *TIME* for all *TRUTHS* to be manifested once more.

They should be listened to, or else we shall have to sleep in ignorance, again waiting for another *NEW ERA* to come and wake us up.

*Our Biggest Sin
Is Ignorance.*

A Short History of Meditation

Meditation is a Spiritual Science brought back to us by the Masters.

Such a Master, *Mahavatar Babaji* gave the Pure Meditation, of which I speak here, to *Lahiri Mahasaya* his disciple, to teach to all in India, to those people who wished to become Self–Realized, or, felt a desire to go forward within themselves. This was, as far as we know, the first time it had been bestowed on a house-holder.

For Pure Meditation is always bestowed lovingly and should not be bestowed with intellect only.

From Lahiri Mahasaya it was passed on to Sri Yukteswar, and then to my Guru, Paramahansa Yoga-nanda, who was asked to take it to the West.

Pure Meditation is a means whereby one's whole being is concentrated on God – the inner you.

There are many Meditations as there are ideas. The one that I write about mainly here is 'a crown jewel', a Pure Meditation that takes you through all your *LIFETIMES,* in truth, a spiritual 'Do-It-Yourself' kit for all of life's situations.

This Meditation incorporates everything that is needed for you, missing but not *one* important divine truth.

This is but a *taster* read on.

When people became ill they searched to find a cure, hence medicine came into being. When people found life and its pleasures did not bring happiness, they looked around, and within, to find the God of peace and contentment. 'Necessity is the Mother of Invention', and so that is how the Seers of India scientifically searched for, and found out what life and death were all about. In doing so they also discovered how to find peace and happiness, better health, better living; all from the Self–Realization that the Infinite is within us all. No small wonder!

We are all suffering from separation, we are all too busy for God and Self–Realization, so why should the Infinite Power *not* be too busy for us – to feed us?

Man has the gift of reason and thought. These Seers had tried to find happiness and God with their five senses; but not being able to do this, they then closed the five senses and went inwards, concentrating more deeply, to find out if a Higher Intelligence behind life existed. As they inwardly concentrated more, so the wisdom within provided all the answers to the questions they had pondered on, thus converting conceptions of God into perceptions of God.

It has taken many years for the meditative East to reach the West, and for the material West to reach the East; both learning something from each other. There are two paths to the Infinite, the outer active, and the inner stillness which is Meditation, comprising of many forms. Both paths are necessary.

This Pure Meditation has only come back into being during the century before last to help everyone obtain Self–Realization in one lifetime. It includes mind pranayama, breath control, and the essentials from all Yoga techniques. It needs time and patience, and a desire to know yourself. It is one of the oldest forms of meditation known, and although once lost, has been brought back through a lineage of Self–Realized Masters. It has been perfected for the demands of life in our time.

If you follow faithfully all that you are taught in this Meditation, then you will find you have become more liberated and a happier person, drawing all of life's gifts to you, and above all the knowledge that the Universal Christ Consciousness lies within you all.

GURUS AND MASTERS REFLECT GOD –

AND LIFE EXAMPLES TO FOLLOW

'TIL WE BECOME ONE.

Meditation: Realization and Mastery of Self

Meditation is an all embracing word, but in its entirety it means, focusing and thinking on one special thought, thing or sound. It is most important to do this for any spiritual progress, for to Meditate properly — makes us aware of our ego, thus allowing us to deal with it. It brings us wisdom, spirituality, love, and in time to come, fulfils our every need.

For those who want to progress within themselves, to find the Realization of Self and their Creator, Meditation cannot be omitted.

There are many different forms as there are individuals, as mentioned, so the Meditation must be found for the person in question, taking into account their 'life style', and their (at present) capabilities or evolutionary state.

A person must desire to progress spiritually and wish to Meditate before one can begin with them. If the desire is very real within, then one is guided to a Guru~Master who knows of the 'pitfalls', and can help the progress of that person.

The guidance to a Master may be directly, or indirectly through those closely associated with them.

We are speaking of Meditation for those who are earnestly seeking the 'spiritual path', but if everyone in every walk of life, put Meditation into practice, but for a short while each day, they would then find not only their health and peace of mind improving, but also the material – jobs, finance, and their personal relationships.

FOR THE SPIRITUAL PATH YOU NEED:

DESIRE

PATIENCE

DEVOTION

WHICH IN TURN WILL HELP YOU FIND YOUR INTUITION,

THEN ALL ELSE WILL FOLLOW NATURALLY.

Pure Meditation and Meditations

In every cell and part of us may we feel the joy and peace within us of our Meditation.

To Meditate means to think – concentrate on one particular given thing.

This Pure Meditation incorporates all the Yogas. It is The Raja Yoga, which means 'King of Yogas': It is also Kriya Yoga and it is beautiful, powerful and true.

Once you start calling anything or anyone by a Name, it becomes *that thing* or *person,* leaving little room for anything else; therefore I prefer not to name this Meditation *exclusively* but to call it 'Pure Meditation' thereby leaving room for its expansion of truth.

There are many forms of Yoga, techniques which quicken the act of Self~God~Realization.

YOGA means *UNION* and a Yogi is one who practices one of the scientific techniques of Yoga – whatever their status in life, be it married or otherwise.

Bhakti Yoga   Is the Spiritual approach to God. It stresses all-surrendering love as the principal for communication and union with God.

Jnana Yoga   Is the path through transmutation of the discriminative power of the intellect, into the omniscient wisdom of the soul.

Laya Yoga   The absorption of the mind in the perception of certain astral sounds.

Karma Yoga   Is the path through non–attached action and selfless service. Giving the fruits of one's actions to The Infinite as The Doer. Through this path the devotee becomes free of ego and experiences God.

Mantra Yoga   This is communion obtained through devotional concentrated repetition of root words. Sounds that have a spiritual beneficial vibratory potency.

Hatha Yoga   Is a system of techniques and physical postures (asanas) that promote health and mental calm, thus paving the way to realization.

Raja Yoga   This some say is the Royal or highest path to God, and includes the highest essentials from all other forms of Yoga. It teaches scientific Meditation.

Kriya Yoga   Is union with the Infinite Beloved through a given act – of breaths.

All these given Yogas are well worthwhile, but if we take the Raja Yoga and the Kriya Yoga (which are in Pure Meditation) with its breaths, changes and charges our blood and body with new life – purified prana and oxygen: then surely those two put together will produce one of the best Meditations, the Kriya 'One

Breath' being bestowed when the Meditator is ready for it , and not before.

This is why, though Meditation can be taught from written lessons, (not books) under the guidance of evolved spiritual souls, it has always been better to seek out a Guru, who has been given the right by their Guru to teach and guide people in Meditation.

Gurus are Self/God~Realized souls, *(Gu)* to dispel *(Ru)* darkness. They can help you to dispel your darkness and ignorance, blessing you, giving you their unconditional love, so that *in turn* you become of love and light.

Gurus are taken lightly these days. You hear of Gurus of film, of finance, of this, of that and the other, but this is only said out of ignorance of not knowing of *their* true part in life. These people must not be condemned in our thoughts, but only forgiven in the hope that their ignorance will eventually be dispelled.

Gurus/Masters though they teach, their ways are different from ours, for they are at one with the Universe and God.

They mirror you, when you see and speak with them. They *reflect* what you are – to yourself, so you will see the truth. But at all times showing you unconditional love. Isn't that wonderful, and worth waiting for your true Guru to come?

We normally have to go through the fires of life, from birth to maturity, before we are ready for a Guru.

We need to feel a true desire, at least to look at *ourselves*, when we get this desire, which unsettles us, sometimes making us unknowingly discontent, then and only then, can we meet our 'dispeller of darkness'.

Not all disciples will recognise their Guru, but the Guru always recognises them and will go for years, sometimes lifetimes, waiting for this disciple to ask them for guidance... Up the hill... where there is beauty, but also pitfalls of rocks that only one who has trodden THAT PATH can know about.

If you find such a person and can give them your love and devotion, they will surely light your way to Self–Realization and God–Realization; but it takes two, you know. So many think the Guru should do everything for them – which means – at that time – that very little *can* be done for them.

THEY DISPEL FEAR

WORRY

IGNORANCE

WHEREBY YOU RECEIVE LOVE, PEACE

AND WEALTH OF MIND.

'Seek ye first the kingdom of heaven and all shall be added to you.'

Which simply means find the heaven within your-selves and this will open the doors to *all else*.

Of course we need varied books, and many *teach* us, before we reach this point in time – each has a part to play in our life, but do not mistake the teacher for the Guru; you will know this by the stillness of their eyes, the body and hands do not move in pointless gestures, always taking their time to answer questions.

LET INTUITION BE YOUR GUIDE

SEEK AND YE SHALL FIND

YOUR OWN DISPELLER.

Why Meditate?

Bodies fed on bread – food alone would die.
Cosmic Energy keeps and gives us life.

Let us continue with this reason, why we should put Meditation into our life? Making it as important as having breakfast, reading the newspaper or watching TV.

You notice I say put it *INTO YOUR* life.

Most people separate themselves in their life by thinking that prayer, going to Church or Meditation are a weekly, monthly or maybe once a year activity. Why? Surely we didn't create ourselves. Do we really believe we could build such a beautiful working body as we all possess? Every part of our body knowing exactly what to do and when to do it? Did we fashion our eyes, hair, contour of body, again *NO*.

There is a higher Divine Power that created us and feeds us with the Prana of life. If we want this life force to continue feeding us, guiding us and loving us, should we not, then, think about giving it 'house room'.

We need food for our bodies, but we also need food for our mind and spirit.

Our bodies need food, though not so much as we normally eat. It needs exercise to help keep it strong and supple. The mind needs a different activity.

One, nevertheless, that stimulates, bringing to us a good, healthy, active mind.

The spirit needs its food also, though in this case, to get our *much needed* food, we need time to sit and walk in the peace – by ourselves. We need to commune with our Higher Selves~God~and nature.

The one sentence that is always forthcoming when I say this to people attending lectures is 'I have *no* time.' 'Fine,' then my answer is, 'why should God have time for you, listen to you, look after your every need?'

While most of the people in this world lack peace, patience, have anger and intolerance within them, criticise others instead of looking to themselves, while they are in any of these states, then it is only common sense to see that they will make *themselves* suffer. For 'what you sow, so you reap'.

What makes people like this, comes into another chapter, but what helps towards these 'bad habits' which they truly are, is too much television, the high frequency energy given off from the multi-dotted screen can and does have very adverse effects upon us.

Overeating, continuously, takes the energy away from the brain to the stomach and lower areas. This is why eating late at night can cause nightmares, for the spiritual high energy wishes to be free while we sleep, while the digestive juices and process of digestion keeps us earth-bound. Too much food *contributes* to make us *gross* in every sense of the word.

Drugs of any kind have side effects. Sometimes we must take prescription drugs for a given condition that a Doctor is helping us with, but other than that, we should keep away from drugs. We cannot be our true selves, or know what we are truly like, while taking these drugs that alter our very nature. Through the practise of Pure Meditation we will one day be able to reach the state of being able to manage our health ourselves.

I know I am only stating facts maybe already known to most of you, but these truths are worth stating again.

Likewise, alcohol is a drug. A glass of wine with meals occasionally should not harm, but regular intake of wine would make us beholden to it. Spirits likewise do not mix with *the spirit-ual* side of our nature – that we all have, so why take them? They seem to uplift you, only to leave you feeling further from peace and lower in spirit in the next moment.

Is it worth it? In my lifetime I have known so many people who have had all these problems, and yet over-come them with Pure Meditation. Of course, at first, they would not admit to being anything but 'all right', but afterwards, after meditating only for a while, there was a vast improvement. Not only the person in question, but their families and friends were pleasantly amazed at their transformation.

You know the saying, 'We are what we eat'. This is very true.

Paramahansaji, ('ji' is added as a sign of respect) my blessed Gurudeva, also wrote 'We are all a little crazy, but we do not know it, as we always mix with like minded people.' Which once again is true. If we mix with those who do not tell us the truth – then we begin to think that we are right and everyone else is wrong and so forth.

Because of this we must be careful of the company that we keep, *LIKE ATTRACTS LIKE;* and bad habits are extremely difficult to break, so keep to good ones.

If you want to break *any* bad habit or personality trait, do it slowly with a positive mind, affirming you *can* and *will.*

Keep away as much as you can from anyone with that particular trait while you are changing it, and have love and patience with yourself while you are doing it… then you will achieve your goal.

Live Your Truth every minute of your life.
Then your Truth shall make you whole.

Asking.

Asking.

What am I
What are you ~

Simply the most perfectly made and perfected
along with all other beings.
Created from a perfect state and so shall we gain
entry into that perfect state again through
Self–Realization.

Guru's Light

There is a path of light
Guided by the Guru.
There is a path of dark
Lighted by the Guru.

Each step of your way
Nothing done without being Known.
No rest, work… without their knowledge.

You are cradled in love
Looked after each moment of the day.
Kissed by the wind.
Embraced by the sun.
Growing with the rain.
All this Guided by one hand, one heart.
The heart and love of a Guru.

OM

Mind Power ✦ ☽

Two friends met... one said
I think I'm getting a cold... and did.
The other friend said I am NOT getting a cold...
and did not.

The power of the mind is very strong and if we become aware of this, it can change our life.

Depending on the level of *concentration* we have, depends our ability to work well, play well, and allow *it* to change our path in life for the better.

The mind feeds the brain with ideas and thoughts, above this we have a downpouring of a spiritual essence, that, if allowed to work within you – feeds the mind – that feeds the brain. If we do not know, or cannot manifest the Higher Intelligence, then we are left with our mortal thinking that can and does make mistakes.

What the mind thinks hard and long enough, so will it take place...so choose and use an AFFIRMATION best suited to your needs to help with this.

Concentrate on these words saying them night and morning and at other times when needs be.

Say them slowly with full concentration from the heart, finishing wth 'Thy Will be done'.

Keep them short ~ for strength.

Your affirmation will be heard and acknowledged accordingly.

'I just know I must do it' or 'Nothing will change my mind' are statements often heard these days. Why are they so adamant? Probably, because they feel it *INTUITIVELY*. This is the *only* way to know that you are thinking correctly. There is a very thin dividing line between I *know* it (the ego) and I my *SELF* know it (the higher above the mind—*SELF*.) The former is imperfect, the latter perfect because of its source being of a higher level.

To find this intuitiveness, that we all have buried deep within us... and high above us, we need to look at our concentration level. Is it good all the time, or merely when we are doing something that we enjoy? Try concentrating a hundred percent on a subject for ten minutes, see if you can do it. Most think forty percent or sixty percent is a hundred percent, for their lack of knowledge and experience puts them in a deluded state.

Only by being able to concentrate, without any interrupted thought, on any given topic, for any given length of time, can one truly say that one's mind is a hundred percent concentrated.

Intuitiveness is a direct grasp of truth. We can learn to develop this intuitiveness by the given *scientific* techniques used in Pure Meditation.

To have intuition is to have the power to create something that no one else has ever created. It means to try to do things in new ways.

As babies we had that power. Note... the power of a baby deep in thought, playing games as they get older, but, they are not allowed this time to cultivate this powerful state... lunch is ready, nappies to be changed, a friend wants to kiss and cuddle you... so we lose this concentration, we do not *miss* it, for we are not aware of it going, until later on in life. We try to apply ourselves, we can't and then decide we have 'fly by night' minds. 'No' we haven't, we have cultivated a *bad* habit, the way to break this bad habit is not easy, for still we are having demands made on us, of time, at work, of people. It becomes a vicious circle. Now what can we do?, ~once we ask *THAT* question... if with deep concentration it will go into the mind and then into the subconscious, as such, an answer will come, even if not straight away – try it – it works.

My answer to this problem, is making certain I am and *always will be concentrated*, would have to be... learn Pure Meditation or how to go into a meditative state; which is completely different to proper Meditation.

The majority of people do not seem to realise there is a vast difference between MEDITATION and MEDITATIVE STATE, but it will not be long before this knowledge is known worldwide.

Meditative state is a state whereby we can find relaxation, and a level of peace within ourselves by varied use of rituals, words, affirmations and light music. One can become in a meditative state simply by sitting on a hilltop staring into space or listening to beautiful music, or again by listening to someone talking and taking you on a guided visualisation.

These states of the mind are conducive and helpful to everyone.

Practising meditative states helps to calm and peacefullise the inner being and will change us for the better. It is a very important therapy for all who suffer in mind, body or spirit.

Whereby Pure Meditation is a science, it is a scientific and spiritual pathway back to the God *within* you. This path will help you in *every level* of your mind, body and spirit, bringing you eventually, with practice and perseverance, to Self~Realization... God~Realization, and a perfect state of bliss; never again to lose your peace, to be more loving and a much wiser person. Worries are not meaningful any more, they just become part of life, something to work through, to do our best, with full knowledge that we will have learnt much: it will build and strengthen us as nothing else can.

You will be always balanced, *three* times as happy – for you will always be content.

Liken the **soul** to a computer. Pure Meditation gives you the information – which is stored in the soul.

So, by Meditating you can put the question and get your answer.

Heed these words well, for I have, over the years, found this to be *absolute truth;* once more –

'Seek ye the fruits of the Kingdom of Heaven and all shall be added to you.'

No more than one hour a day spent in Meditation will transform your life and those around you. When you think of it, we have twenty four hours to make use of!

Our needs to sleep vary, though five to six hours of good sleep should be ample for most. We have our food to eat to keep our body healthy, then there is work and our play.

How much time do people spend talking to each other, watching television or reading newspapers? Surely there must be a time we can find for *Our Maker,* our helper, *OUR GIVER OF LIFE.*

Times for Meditation

The best times to sit and Meditate are early morning, midday and last thing at night. Though *any time* is worthwhile. We must fit it into our lifestyle, so that it becomes *part* of us… our life.

Try to sit in Meditation before you get too tired. For it's like going to meet a friend – you would not go to see a friend when you are very tired or have not washed, dressed, or shaved. So this rendezvous should be equally, if not more, important to you.

The high divine Infinite power, God, is a friend, the best one you will ever have, this friendship will not only last in this lifetime… but all others: can you truthfully say that of any other friend?

You have to get to know God before you
can love him; when you know God,
you cannot help but love him.

If you do not meditate yet, try sitting quietly in a specially chosen place. Sit comfortably feet on the ground, or cross–legged, hands placed gently, palms up, on your thighs. Take a breath in through the nose – a good deep breath… then sigh the breath out through the mouth. With eyes lightly closed take another breath in and think of the word *PEACE*, then as you breathe out through the nose, see this peace going through your body… down from the top of your head to your arms, hands, spine… whole body… legs and feet. Keep this word *PEACE* in your mind while you continue practising this breath, until you *FEEL AT PEACE*. When the peace comes, stay just a little longer for your body to continue receiving. Always remember to ask for peace at the beginning of this *meditative state*, and give thanks at the end of it.

Infinite Beloved

I thank you.

Help my lotus petals to close

My day to be spiritually guided.

Amen ~ Om.

Remember also to concentrate on the word *PEACE*, do not concern yourself with the in and outward flow of the breath. Just keep in the rhythm of the breath itself.

The degree with which you can focus and concentrate on *THE WORD ONLY*, will determine the outcome of your feelings of peace after practice.

This is a Start… Be at Peace.

God breathes – a word – and a thought – became substance.

Karma Is

I would like to write something on Karma which is a much maligned word, as is Reincarnation.

Karma simply means cause and effect. 'What we sow we reap'. This is why if I see someone doing something not very nice to someone else, I may try to help if wise, but the knowledge is this; that the person that gives suffering to anyone be it by deed or voice will *reap* the same action. It is a just spiritual law that gets activated. It just happens, not necessarily straight away… but sometime… somewhere.

This fact of life is worth noting, if only to make us think, and be careful of what is said, and how we act towards other people.

Every thought we have, will, if we are not careful, produce problems for us.

Here's a true story I would like to share with you.

Many years ago an elderly lady came to stay with us. She could not walk very well and therefore spent a lot of the daytime in her room or the garden.

We had no television. She had informed me how much she missed one. So I prayed that we might get a good large set for her… for there was no money to buy one… within a matter of hours we were offered a twenty-four inch television – wonderful you might think, but it was much too big for her small room. The mistake was asking for a *large* one, not for the set itself.

This was wrong to specifically specify conditions.

The mind is an extremely powerful instrument, particularly when it is coupled with good concentration. We must be careful how we use it.

Cause and effect must start with the individual – each thought goes out like a particle of substance, to be drawn to like substances: e.g. anger will go out into the ether and be drawn to other anger, likewise, love and peace thoughts. It is in our own hands what our family, friends, and even to a degree, what the World is like today.

I heard of a man who slapped his wife's face. She in turn slapped her child; on getting to school, that child hit a playmate and so it can go on. Thought, every action, and every word we speak, goes out somewhere and does something; singly or collectively it matters not, only that there is a cause and effect.

We are part of a whole plan. One piece of a jigsaw puzzle, which is to say we are important... how can this jigsaw be complete without us?

What we do, think and say, has an effect, first of all, on us, then everyone else.

If we think good thoughts, do good deeds, then the World will become a better place. If not... then it will become a worse place for everyone including our children.

CAUSE AND EFFECT

IT IS TRUTH THAT IS WRITTEN HERE

We are but lotus petals made up
of lotus centres.
We dance upon each lotus daily,
and on our way find
that the beauty and colour of each is beyond all
human conception.

Reincarnation

Early Christianity taught reincarnation. Jesus also revealed his Knowledge of this truth, when he said 'Elias' is come already, reincarnated in the body of John the Baptist.

To reincarnate was accepted by the church authorities several hundred years ago. One day the Synod met to discuss its beliefs between the Churches and its followers. They decided that the power of the Church would be lost if people believed in reincarnation; for they would be able to work out their own salvation, themselves, and probably would not see the Priests and their Church as a necessary organisation for their salvation.

Because of these thoughts the Synod took the steps of deliberately leaving out any written material, of the assets of believing *in* reincarnation. It then enabled them to maintain the power and control, that they have always had, over the peoples.

This word reincarnation simply means we are given more than one life time to perfect and make good our mistakes.

Our fall from grace came slowly, from tasting the different fruits (ways) of people and therefore it is going to take lifetimes to *perfect ourselves* again (unless we use the means of Meditation).

There is no death… only life… after life… after life.

Most people have wonderful holidays abroad these days, people travel distances. If your Mother went to live permanently in Africa, and you could not see her – or get to see her – would you then say she was dead?…

Of course she would not be, though she may seem dead, *to you,* if there were no means of any communication. In reality she would be alive, somewhere else, in another part of the Universe.

This is what happens when we pass from this earth plane; we leave our unwanted bodies of cell tissue, to travel to another country (plane).

'There are many mansions in the house of my Father' meaning many different planets and states of being.

Where we ended up would depend on our life styles here. Remembering that 'like attracts like', would we not, then, be with those who were like ourselves, and at the same level of understanding? Yes, we would, and, go to *that plane.*

It does not mean we have had to be paragons of virtue from our birth to death, but simply, that, when we are mature, we try our best to improve and follow the Ten Commandments, which is only common sense, if we do not wish to get into more trouble.

There is no time factor on these planes, there never has been. People here have made time factors for their own convenience. Times to rest, work and play.

In the different mansions there are souls who are teachers, helpers and guides, to those who need their help.

It is important we believe in something before we make this journey, otherwise we may well end up in darkness, waiting for someone to show us a light... love and God.

Everything is beautifully worked out for the best to everyone, so now it is up to us.

Each time we pass, we may rest and learn from higher souls, meet our friends – but one day the feeling of wanting to be reborn again will make itself felt. We are not forced to make *this decision,* but do so because this earth plane, amongst others, is such a good training ground, with all its problems as well as its beauty, the fact we can sense, but not bathe in God's light and love *all* the time... hurts us. We want to get nearer to our Mother/Father, and be forever at *one* with this love and light. This is the strongest reason, alongside perhaps, the reason to help others as well, for coming back. (Once the decision is made we choose the parents or parent who will give us the most chance to learn, *not* necessarily the most perfect ones, who are bright, have money, and a large house, but ones with *their* own problems, that, we will be able to learn from, and from this make progress. When this opportunity arrives with a pregnancy... it is taken, and so another soul is reborn. It can be a new or a very old soul, it doesn't matter – we are here again, we have been given another chance to make good our previous *lives* and mistakes.

Our old memories of our past lives, of our parents, friends, and other happenings are obliterated for our own good. But we do bring our personalities that we never lose, plus our remembrances of our talents back in the superconscious mind, which houses all our thoughts and deeds, through all our life times.

Through all these life times, we are given chances to progress on every level of *ourselves,* the most important one being, in our spiritual self. It is then up to us whether we take those chances or not.

God made us in his likeness. We ARE OF GOD. Our soul is a perfect likeness, and we already have the CHRIST Consciousness within us, but, covered over with layers of wrong living, – so that we have caused a separation from *this state within ourselves…* of our true BEING, and to get it back, we have to strip these layers off… one by one.

Can you visualise an onion with its many skins around it? We have to peel it, before we can get to, and eat of, the onion. Likewise with ourselves.

Let's peel those unwanted skins away, let us get back our peace, love and wisdom. Feeling God's presence… light and bliss. Until we do, the World *will not* be a peaceful one. While we are *separated* from *ourselves,* we can never be completely, and at all times, *at peace.*

This is not religious thinking, but common sense, and proved, by looking around us and seeing the unrest and lack of peace in everyone, everywhere.

God – the Christ power is *within* us and we *can* find it, *who* ever we are, and in whatever walk of life… That is… if, we truly wish to find these *JEWELS* within.

I came to these beliefs and knowledge as an unbeliever.

Brought up in the Church of England, then as a Roman Catholic, I was not allowed such thoughts as these written here, but with time for soul-searching, experiences and such truths being shown me, I now can talk and write with full knowledge that this *is* the truth.

Do not dismiss these words without first – reading books, to open your mind – to think and meditate on, what I have written here. You will then find it out for yourselves, enriching and beautifying your life as you go along.

★

There is a true saying that goes —

The Church can never be more than a willing servant, who can know the mind and will of God, only in proportion to its likeness to him. The purpose and secrets of God are revealed to the individual Souls, not deposited in trust with institutions.

The Act of Marriage

Love that comes from understanding is one of the highest expressions of love.

'More marriages are made on this earth plane, than are made in heaven.'

As we make our own heaven and hell, by the attitudes and beliefs that our minds accept, our negativity or positivity will determine our state of health and being, at any given time.

If anger or bitterness is housed within us... we will not feel happy or very well. If we can be patient and forgiving, without criticism of others, then, no doubt our minds and bodies will be a great deal healthier.

Basically, you might say, negative and positive traits affect us, to the greater extent, more than anything else, so why do we allow them to come, manifest, and create havoc for us?

Our ego and pride are generally at fault here and while the pride and ego are so prominent within us... they will cause problems. We will make mistakes, wrong decisions, cause hurt to others, and make wrong choices in our own relationships, along with marriage.

Separation and divorce have been with us a long time. We choose partners sometimes, when we are too young to make a good decision. Other times it can be on a very physical level only. Sometimes it is for companionship, or maybe it is just so one can leave home.

There are a variety of reasons, but it makes me wonder how much time is given to really studying each other, and asking ourselves if some of the most important attributes are truly there in your partner... that need to be there... for you.

Of course there usually is a physical attraction to a degree, though more important than that, are, the beliefs of the mind and spirit of both the partners.

I do not think long engagements are always a good idea... for that state can become stale to both. But the belief that two people, desiring a marriage, should study and get to know each other very well, is very important.

My Mother used to 'vet' my boy friends, asking – do they show respect? Are they good losers?, Have a sense of humour? And can they take a joke against themselves? Some good points. Though we all know it is the small things in marriage that seem to upset the most.

Perhaps one of the *most* important areas to look at is, can you talk and discuss *anything* with each other?... I mean, *anything* and *everything*.

Having had a great deal to do with matrimonial problems, I would say that an inability to discuss, plus selfishness, are two of the biggest marriage breakers.

Marriages made in heaven (or the *wisest* Spiritual part of our innermost self) are more rare, and they will sustain a full lifetime 'til one or the other passes on.

With marriages between two people that have been chosen unwisely, then, there is usually a parting between them somewhere in their lifetime, even if they try to work at their marriage for given periods of time. The reason for this state is that each person is meant *to* evolve and go forward… if either, one or the other, in the marital status prevents this happening, then the true spiritual law comes into being… the marriage must and will break, allowing each partner to continue to go forward, – each in their own way to fulfil their future path in this lifetime.

What about our vows then. Well, yes, we should try to keep our vows, but not at the cost of other lives. The broken marriages could be called more like partnerships gone wrong, and should be seen as such. Everyone, possibly, makes one big mistake in a lifetime. We should look at it in this light.

Sorting out our life, properly, during this traumatic time of parting, is a most important time in our lives. What we do, and how we do it, will not only shape our life, but others' as well.

The sign, of separating or divorcing properly, and justly, is that everyone will benefit from the parting in due course.

To know if we are doing the best possible, can only be known by *intuitively* following our innermost feelings – it's a *knowing* that *come what may*, it must *be done*.

Marriage is a very beautiful state.

We must not be black and white on this subject, or bury our heads in the sand. Look at each problem as it comes along, face it, deal with it.

Everyone we meet teaches us something, and we in turn teach them, we meet and are put together to learn from each other, but when those lessons are learnt – we have a choice, of staying or going, keeping our relationship with friends or not.

My Mother suffered greatly in her first marriage. She was forced to marry a man who had money and status, but he drank and abused her, causing her to have several miscarriages. Being a Roman Catholic, she obeyed her Priest of the Church, who ordered her to return each time she went to him for help. I have written on this in my book *Come*.

That she married my Father, and then love was forever with them, was wonderful, but – that people, from ignorance, suffer – is not.

Where dogma lies
Truth does not.

Breath of Help

Sit comfortably, the eyes closed, hands folded, watching the breath come and go. Do not force any change of breathing only watch it quietly coming… and going, then with eyes opened, gaze at a picture or photo of Jesus, Buddha, someone special, and ask for their help… to know what to do. Keep concentrated on this until you feel a sense of peace. Stay as long as you need to. Then give thanks and go about your day.

Do this night and morning. In the middle of the day as well if you wish.

Keep doing this until you *feel* and know, intuitively the Answer.

You **will** receive this help.

In **God's time**

not

your time

A Path in Life

INTUITION IS THE DIRECT GRASP OF TRUTH
IN ITS ENTIRETY.

Everyone has a pathway in their lifetime, be it simply called a skeleton or a blueprint. That is why sometimes one can hear other people say 'I do not think *this* job is for me' or '*No*, that's not for me'.

We know ourselves. Our higher, wiser self knows everything about us. We also have an appel and repel action built within us; if we go against *that* inner knowledge, for whatever reason, we suffer.

Now, there is a time to have problems and suffer, for, from these we progress and learn. But here, I mean the times people take work, friendships and enjoyment for the wrong reason; e.g. money, fame, for 'kicks' maybe. We cannot fool God... only ourselves... some of the time... but not all of the time.

Follow your path, be it what you *want* or not. It may be just what you *need* for the now, and because of this reason only, you will feel at peace within, though outwardly, you may have a moan.

I had to take many varied types of work. While working at them I often wondered...*why?* Later I found out that all the different jobs I had taken, helped build me into what I am today, utilising *all* the skills learnt on my way (*in Mata Yogananda's book* Come - A Spiritual Journey).

It was not an easy time for me, yet, I would not be without those experiences. Those opportunities helped me start a Centre, keep accounts, have a family and much more.

Be yourself, go with life. Let it give… to you… and guide you… for that is God's way.

Keep as peaceful as you can within. Think well before you act. Ask inwardly for help… wait… 'til you feel a *surge* to go ahead.

The plan of life is too vast for us to see the whole; we are not expected to do so. Our shoulders are not strong enough to take more than one day at a time… one minute at a time.

The whole picture is known by the Infinite Beloved. You may be asked to suffer, to gain experience, to help others and… yourself, but the outcome will be perfect for everyone and the evolution of *all*.

Over the years I have found perfect truth in following the above procedure. Never once has it failed me, though often I may have failed myself with lack of complete trust in the entire Divine Plan.

Follow your own path.
Be still and at peace.
Know that you are God.

Do your best for each day.
Do not think of tomorrow.
What you do this minute, makes the next,
and what you do today...
makes your tomorrow.

Intellect, Intelligence and Common Sense

When you try to perceive within,
the door is opened to you,
in accordance to your ability
Your ability of being still and knowing you ARE.

We cannot find peace, love and God through the intellect. The intellect thinks, cuts, dissecting everything in pursuit of the truth, but God's truth is evasive *in* its diversity, *no* dogma, black or whiteness, only panoramic views, ever changing.

The most difficult students are those who think that by having intellect, they are going to be the first ones to find Self/God~Realization. They read numerous books on the subject, go to lectures, debate by the hour, with people of the same, or lesser knowledge. They then believe they are wise. They become a walking encyclopedia – no more.

I am not condemning intellect as such, it is a good facility to have within us, but to find out inner truths, we need to put the intellect on the 'shelf', while we turn to our intelligence and common sense.

With intelligence we can tackle most situations, we sort and sift *more* from the heart area, so eventually getting a more correct definition of the spiritual aspect of ourselves. Couple intelligence with common sense and they make a perfect vehicle for finding the God within.

Books should still be read, lectures and people listened to naturally, but our discussion ratio is lower, and our inner thinking and 'musing' things over the greater. Such people are more inclined to ask for help, pray that they may see the light on such matters… and it works.

I remember when very young sitting by the side of a fireplace crying and crying, asking why I didn't have intellect… no doubt someone had commented on this to me… My Mother lovingly said, 'You have intelligence and common sense, use them well, and that is all you will need, not everyone needs to be intellectual'. I dried my eyes and though not understanding completely, felt much relief. Now I understand what she was saying to me.

No, I have not needed intellect, but I have always needed intelligence and common sense – we all need these. I leave intellect to those who need it… as scientists and others do.

Once you have found peace, love, humility, and are master or mistress over yourself, then, if you have intellect, it can be taken back, off the shelf, and be put to good use. So you see intellect is not being decried. I am simply saying, it does get in *our* way… at times.

A Story Told

There was a dog, cat, flea, horse, lion and bird
that took the paths through to fear,
went on to the path of peace, Love, then
on the path of Self–Realization –
and finally to Om.

The only one that did not reach Om
was the flea, as it could never BE STILL.

Animals

We are all born out of one love.

Some people say they love animals but not humans. Others say they love humans, but not animals. How can this be? We are *all* full of God's life force that sustains us and feeds us.

The problem is the expectancy that we should be loved and liked: be able to treat people and animals as we feel we want to, at that moment; and then that they in turn will not mind, or at least, understand why we are doing it – how self-centred these thoughts are.

Animals should be treated *as* animals with respect, with love, though with insight, that they can kick, bite or scratch but only if humans treat them, as *humans*. They do not like such treatment, resent it, and show the resentment in the only way they know how.

Have you ever watched an over-loving person with their cat or dog? – kissing them, tickling them, picking them up, putting them down briskly, pushing them out of doors, when the animal would rather stay in!

Some cats and dogs can get tired of this treatment and retaliate in their own way – and then we get upset.

Reverse the given situation in your own mind, and you will see what I mean.

'Animals are so much *easier* to get on with'; is a constant saying. They do know the hand that feeds them, and they are clever enough not to bite that hand, unless provoked too much.

All God's creatures have a part to play in life, a useful purpose, but like humans, animals also have their faults.

Our evolutionary status is higher than an animal's. We have the Christ Consciousness within us, enabling us to have a high degree of spiritual wisdom which we can strengthen through knowing and helping all animals, but please do not forget the human beings, that so need our love.

When it is time for our friends – the animals – to pass, they go on to other various planes of life, depending on whether they have lived with human beings or have lived out in the wild. They can return to a *Collective* energy. Their Spirit~energy can take a form for a period of time to be with us and for us to learn

Very like us, when they pass, all the illnesses and physical disabilities that they had on this earth planet, will disperse, as they shed their cellular bodies.

If the love between animal and human has been a deep and caring one, then they will in all probability meet again. Our desire to meet them again will bring about a reunion, be it in our dream state or, when we pass over.

When young I had to have my Springer Spaniel put to sleep. He was suffering greatly. Many vets tried to help him to better health, but to no avail. He remained constantly in my mind and thoughts… wondering if there was life after death (for then I was ignorant on any such matters) I would pray, to be shown what happened to such animals, until – later on in my life, one night I visited him in the state between wakefulness and dreaming. He was very happy, living with my mother, who loved all animals, and though when he was on this earth plane his coat was rough and ill with eczema, now his coat was shining… like it had never shone before. The meeting was mutually loving. We shared what seemed like a few moments, and then we both went our separate way, each knowing, that this had to be – for the present.

What a revelation that was to me. I have seen him since, but I know now, without any doubt, that he and all animals like him are lovingly looked after. We need never worry, God and the spiritual law would not allow otherwise, though while we have them with us here, let us try to understand them. Be firm, but loving, and give them space to develop in their *own* way. Creatures are very knowing, with little going on escaping their notice. Respect them for this. For they are all God's creatures.

Not one sparrow shall fall,
without this knowledge
being known by me.

Babies... Children

In my Father's house are many mansions. If it were not so I would have told you. I go to prepare a place for you.

St. John Ch.14 v.2

There is so much more information I would like to be able to give you... much more... than I am able to here. Fortunately this information can be gained through the Mother Centre's Pure Meditation Course which covers all these subjects fully.

For now it will have to suffice, to barely cover the groundwork, but it is nevertheless very important to know what happens to babies and children, in the Karma (cause and effect) and reincarnation situation.

If a baby is born, with what the medical profession call a congenital disease, that child must have knowledge of this happening before it lodges itself in the womb of it's mother. The baby must need this condition to progress in some way (cause and effect), which only God and baby know. The remembrance of this truth will be obliterated before the child is born.

Children are not like adults, in the given sense, that they have the facility of greater acceptance of bodily pain, they still have great faith in going along with life's situations and problems. That is not to say they do not suffer at all, but they do not suffer to the degree that the adult does; we are conditioned in our *minds* towards pain, babies are not. They do cry for attention if they are hungry or have a soiled nappy, but surely that is the *only* way they can communicate at that present stage in their life.

Babies with a disease, depending on kind and severity, will then either get better, or pass on to another plane (plane is a place… a level of) – an energy field where without any doubt, they are loved, and looked after, by whomever they need the most. They can be reborn quite quickly again, though more often than not, they will stay to continue their growing and learning.

As was previously stated, there is no time factor there, so babies could remain babies for a much longer period than they would here, or, take up their *many facets* from their previously lived life times, and then they would be living at their most spiritual level they will have attained to. The only reason we meet them in our various levels of dream states, is so that the love tie is never broken. We are aware of them growing. Though our conscious level does not always remember these meetings… our superconsciousness does remember, so that when we pass over and meet them again, we are not total strangers to each other.

This reunion only takes place if *we* want it to – by desire and love.

My held belief is, that there is life energy in the womb: from the time the seed is sown… and it is implanted in the lining of the mother's womb. The personality of this child may *not* be there, or the human characteristics, but *GOD'S LIFE ~ ENERGY IS.*

An aborted baby, like one in a miscarriage, still, will learn, from its short experience of conception and the time within the womb. Maybe, that is all it needs before returning to its Maker… and be received with open arms by a spiritual soul who will love and care for them.

I have lost a baby… I know the feelings that *churn* up within us, of doubt and guilt, but I shall write more of that in a moment.

Let us now look at children who are older, have grave physical or mental problems, and pass over.

How often have we seen these children smiling or just quietly accepting, the fact, that they have only a little longer here. They often have a built-in calmness about their beings, and within.

Most are inwardly *aware* of the situation, even if words are not spoken, 'that their time has come'. It is like a message being given inwardly and with great tenderness, so there is no unnecessary jarring to the soul on departure.

The body when in pain always looks worse in it's suffering than it really is, but we do not realise this because the outer signs can be horrific to our mortal eyes.

Inwardly, it is a different matter, unbeknowingly, a spiritual type of ether is forming, cutting off areas of knowing, within the brain. This happens with suicide, muggings, killings, torture, rape and other such ordeals. One day this will be scientifically proved.

God does help.

Even if it does not always seem so to us.

Having lost a baby, I was privileged to experience meeting, many times with my son, and have learnt many lessons. But still *God only* knows all.

When this life ends
and there is no tomorrow,

We need to be ready for, The Journey.

A few things, only are needed,
An honesty ticket to take you on.

A peace WITHIN, *making light,*
to shed the darkness.

And above all, Trust; for your journey.

How Do We Meet
With Souls Passed On

It is in the 'Infinite Beloved's hands'.

We must not and cannot demand – for nothing will come of that demand.

We can ask each night before we sleep to meet, always finishing with

'Thy Will Be Done'

do not worry or fret, just wait, if you need this meeting, to help you in some way, it will be allowed in the heavens (other planes) and you will have your wish granted.

God will answer your needed call.

By scientific and spiritual techniques, we can also meet others. This is how sometimes I meet the Masters, Jesus, and my Gurudeva Paramahansaji. But this is not used lightly, and we must obey the spiritual laws (which we also teach at the Centre).

Our spiritual all-seeing eye in our forehead, the seat of Christ Consciousness, must be awake usually for this to happen… but then I have known people in great need, who had Jesus appear to them, and it has changed their lives.

There can be no black and white or dogma here, for all is possible, if only we could accept… that all will be allowed by God… if we follow the commandments of life.

If we are blind we cannot see.

But it does not mean, there Is Nothing to see.

*If we cannot See without glasses
we put them on… and can see.*

*We need our Spiritual glasses
to see more.
And therefore*

we must not feel guilt if we lose a baby, but look at the reason behind it.

It is what is in our minds that matters, why it happened? or with abortion, why we allowed it to happen?

If we worry… we suffer, not the baby.

Give the departed baby a name, and know it is alive and well, loving you.

Speak to her or him, until you feel they have heard you, then wait for the peace to come.

Remember there can be no ill feelings from the baby, only those that you make for yourself.

*Don't do it –
Don't fret.
Remember, love,
And live your life.*

Through Pure Meditation we get to know the truth, on all matters, for ourselves. Once we know that we are important to the whole of creation and have God *within* us, we can start taking our rightful place as sons and daughters of God ~ Creation.

Jesus, Buddha, Krishna to name but a few sons of God. They became at *ONE* with their Father – so there was no separation.

We must not get carried away with the ignorance of not seeing who we truly are... sons and daughters each equal as to our beliefs and thoughts.

We are here to work our way back from the separation we have made from our lifetimes, back to being at one with our Infinite Beloved friend... God.

With reincarnation and karma being a fact, we cannot help but know that God is pure... of love and light, giving us many chances to get back our birthright that we have lost.

With Pure Meditation we can be master or mistress of ourselves, with these scientific and spiritual techniques we can learn how to do *just this*... to keep ourselves happy and healthy. This is no dream, but a wakeful state of knowledge. We have never needed it so much as we do today.

If we believe that only others can bless us, get to know *GOD*, be good enough to deserve God's Love, then we cannot be as wise as we should be.

There are no favourites here and in truth, only in the world of 'make believe' – in our ignorant thinking.

Your life is in *your own* hands, no one else's. It always has been so, we can do and become anything we want to become, providing that we have the power of concentration, and desire to do so. There is a scientific and spiritual way to learn how to do this *in Pure Meditation.*

Many people prefer to put their lives into other people's hands. They feel it is easier... less responsibility for them to shoulder, or maybe they feel it is *not* possible to do those things which I state here. I understand this thinking, though do not agree with it, for it simply is not true.

In my lifetime I have gone from letting others tell me what is best for me, to finding out what is best for *myself.*

I am in charge of myself.

If I can do this... you also can do it. If one person can... *two* can, three can... we *all can,*

with God's help.

Look at the World around you, at the trees, animals, the seasons. The beauty is there for our eyes to behold. It's for us to do with as we see fit? – *No!* – The World

Mata Yogananda Mahasaya Dharma

Swami Sri Yukteswarji

Lahiri
Mahasayaji

Ji Jesus

Babaji

Paramahansa Yoganandaji ~
Mata Yoganandaji's Guru

Mata Yoganandaji with some of her disciples

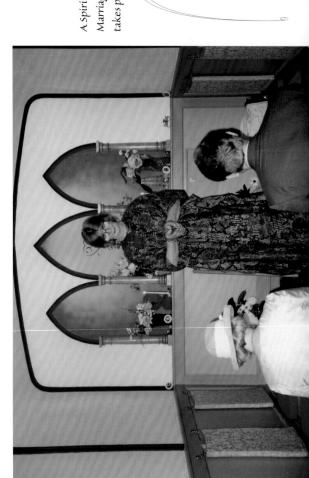

A Spiritual
Marriage
takes place

The Mahasaya Room. For the timeless teachings.

A Centre for Meditation.
Knowledge sets you free.

is perfectly made to suit all human beings. We are the ones who structure and change buildings, forests, landscapes, and I believe some of us are at fault with the changes that we are bringing about, not only in this capacity, but also in our own daily lives and given situations that we meet.

Changes start with us, at home; we must be responsible for ourselves, and those around us.

The World will not change for the best by leaving it to others...

It will change as we change... *within* ourselves. That is the quickest, surest way of changing all situations within the family, and in the World at large.

You have no doubt come across some people who make you feel restless, others make you smile or feel happy being with them. These people are reflecting out the energy of light or darkness (anger or peace) that they have around them. It's in the air and we pick it up or absorb it – as a sponge absorbs liquids... another form of energy.

If we go into a room where there has been, or are, disagreeable people, we can pick up the atmosphere and feel uneasy. A happy house, we can detect right away.

Have you ever sat next to a person for a while, then, when it is time to leave, you have gone home feeling tired and drained? You have allowed that person access to the energy around you. Fortunately, that does not happen very often, but do you see how very important it is for us to have knowledge, and be *in charge* of ourselves? So this cannot happen.

We are made up out of the atoms of the life force (prana). The atoms have, and are, energy, that sustain the life within us. We are made in God's image (Christ's power within us) and we are of mind, body and spirit. We have many levels, but for now let us look at the fact that we have a duplicate of ourselves called the Etheric around us. This counterpart goes with us when we pass. This Etheric contains a spiritual spine that houses all our spiritual vessels necessary for our progress, vortices of energy (chakras – on our pathway to God)… exit… and entry. Around this shadow of ours, is the Auric, which means an emanation of what we feel and are, at any one given moment of time. We give off emanations of anger, peace, love, happiness, but likewise we can also absorb with it, the expression 'they are in my space' is a good one, for it happens. If a person is very sensitive and aware, they can feel strongly any invasion of *their space*.

What can we do about it? Well, firstly, be more aware of what sort of mood people are in, when they are around you! Note and make an inward verbal affirmation that you will not allow entry of that mood – that energy. Then see yourself surrounded by light, make the sign of the cross (The Cross means that you believe in God and know that God's help is there for you) or just ask that you may be fully protected – and then go in faith.

If you are visiting or being visited by someone who causes you to get 'uptight' and irritable, cross your arms over your solar plexus while you are talking.

This is a very good practical way of stopping entry or exit of unwanted energies. But, afterwards, gain more knowledge of yourself and why you allow the giving and taking to happen.

So much information is to hand these days on such matters, all so very necessary for our own peace of mind.

Now you know how to conserve your energy if giving and receiving, why not try knowing your true Self.

Sit on a chair with legs uncrossed, or on the floor with legs crossed. Keep the back and spine as straight as possible. Hands upturned on top of thighs, near the abdomen. Close your eyes. Take a breath in through the nose and sigh it out of the mouth. Do this three to four times, then still with closed eyes, think of a very spiritual person, a Saint, a Master (They are at one with God's Peace and Love), some soul who you can love and relate to. Think of them, and now ask them that you may be given the chance to look properly at yourself, and be guided, if needs be, to someone who can help you, – that you will accept anything shown to you. Sit at peace, remaining still, thinking of this person –

when your mind starts to wander – let it do so, but only on yourself.

When you feel it is time to stop, regardless of whether you have received or not, give thanks to that person, ask for the love and light to surround you. Then after sitting for a few more moments, get up and *continue your day,* in the knowledge that in the correct place and at the right time you will receive your answer.

It cannot be demanded, only asked for lovingly and with patience – for who knows better – than a wiser soul.

When you try to perceive within,
The door is opened to you, in accordance to your ability,
Your ability of being still and knowing you ARE.
When you can feel you ARE, then the Great awareness of God within is possible.

The Breath of Life

Pure Meditation will teach us how to breathe properly, and use the science of breathing to our advantage.

In our everyday life we accept breathing as a fact, one that establishes that we are still living. We are breathing in oxygen – so we must be alive.

But are we fully alive in our mind, body and spirit? The fact is that very few people know how to breathe properly, taking in fully their daily requirements of oxygen.

We hear of the Fakirs who can bury themselves for days under the earth in a vessel of some kind, and live to tell the tale. They are not breathing oxygen in while buried. They have used one of the Kriya breaths to stop all bodily organs and systems functioning, whereby they hold themselves in a state of complete rest. Because, in this state, the body is not working, and the cells are not reproducing, there is a state of no–decay and the Fakir is living on the prana within, and can come back to a bodily living condition whenever he wishes to do so.

Everyone needs oxygen to feed their bodily needs. Though, our spiritual essence lives on prana, which is in the air as well as in our bodies, but is made of a much lighter substance and protein. Once this leaves our body, we are truly, not alive any longer. One only has to think of cases in the newspaper, in the past, or maybe in our own experience, when a person stops breathing, they are taken for dead, but resume breathing in time to prove that they are not: the prana has been sustaining them, keeping them alive. Obviously their life span had not been finished – for we do have a life span, each and every one of us.

Prana is a cosmic energy which surrounds and infuses our human body.

The World was brought into being with... *THE WORD* and cosmic energy – vibration keeps us and the whole World alive. This vibrating energy surrounds not only everyone but everything in creation.

In the beginning was the Word,
and the Word was with God,
and the Word was God.

The same was in the beginning with God.

All things were made by Him;
and without Him was not anything made
that was made.

In Him was life; and the life was the light of men.

And the light shineth in darkness;
and the darkness comprehended it not.

St. John Ch.I v.1–5

We can, with knowledge obtained, use this cosmic life force to energise, harmonise, and enhance ourselves in every possible way, by using our will and concentration to bring more prana into ourselves through *spiritually* designated areas. This can only be done properly with obtained knowledge from a Guru, or a person who is near to being Self-Realized – a person of high spiritual quality that has been chosen to teach and guide in Kriya Yoga.

It is essential to have learnt the art of Pure Meditation before you can try these breaths, as it needs a certain depth of understanding and spiritual awareness, before you will be able to absorb, and do them sufficiently well enough, to enable you to get maximum benefit from them.

But, we can look to our oxygen intake, and learn how to expand our lungs to allow more breath in. Our lungs are like 'bellows'. The harder you pump bellows the more air they produce. The more we expand our lungs, the more air, we can take and produce.

Many conditions are caused or made worse by our inability to breathe properly.

It is only common sense to see that we are aware of how to breathe properly so that, though we may not be wise enough to practice our breath intake daily, we do have the knowledge, and can apply it to ourselves, when we feel it is needful and positive to do so.

The following breaths will help you make a start —
Stand with your feet slightly apart, arms by your side.
Now take a breath in, and as you do so raise your arms
slowly to above your head, on breathing out, slowly
lower them down to your side, in time with your
breath, do this three to five times.

Then the next day do this same progressive breath
A, and then follow it with B:

Stand with feet slightly apart, hands over your ribs,
just on the lower ribs and slightly under. Expand your
hand to cover the two areas. With eyes closed, breathe
in, and as you do so, put a gentle pressure, with your
fingers on the gap (between the floating ribs) feel your
ribs extend out… sideways. Do not pressurise them,
gently help them. As you breathe out relax your hands,
'til the next breath. Do this several times to start with,
then stop, for the extra breath intake may make you feel
dizzy to begin with, until you can build up the capacity
of your lungs.

These breaths are best practised outside or by an
open window.

Please check with your Doctor if you have any
health problems before you use them.

This is not a book on exercises, but we are as 'young
as our spine' with its flow of fluid and with two nerv-
ous systems going out from the spine, it needs to be
kept as supple as possible working with the life flow.

Hatha Yoga will help you to keep supple if you are not good at applying yourself to exercises at home. But do go to a good teacher to learn, as all good exercises can be bad for you, if you do not learn them properly.

May your body be strong
your heart be still
In your 'eye' there be light.

For that is God's will.

The Power of the Mind

We must realise the fact that our minds are makers of all grief and misery as well as all peace and happiness.

We start thinking thoughts which our mind accepts. It's in the conscious mind, and if we give the thought power, it goes out as an energy, collecting like energy along the way, out there, in the ether.

If you send out bad energy... one day it will *boomerang* back to you, if good energy, positive, happy thoughts, go out in depth, then they likewise come back to you.

We have to be very careful, indeed, of what we *do, think or say,* if it is in any way criticism or harmful to others.

These thoughts of positivity and negativity, good or bad, collect as clouds... unseen by mortal eyes, and must, eventually go and do something, somewhere. We are partly responsible for the cloud and therefore, certainly, partly responsible for the world at large.

EACH PERSON CUTS ONE TREE DOWN

IN A LARGE FOREST.

THE FOREST IS NO MORE.

WHO IS RESPONSIBLE?

This is a very good spiritual law, after all, if I criticise someone all the time, that someone, will more likely than not *feel* this criticism, and criticise me… for criticising them. A very just law and providing we accept, this Law, *this truth,* then we will think twice, before we speak, or act in a degrading way to anyone else.

When I found this truth out for myself, in my teens, my feeling, of having the capacity to be mistress of myself once more, was one of extreme gratitude and desire to improve myself, and thereby – a little of the world.

With our will power and concentration, we can control and change ourselves for the better; make our will power into divine dynamic will power. The difference can be noticed straight away, for your life will start changing for the best, and if it's good already, it will be even better still.

The secret of success
is complete
continuity and constancy
of purpose.

Reflection

One day I saw a beautiful swan~like bird.
It was perched high upon a moss covered wall;
its plumage was so pure white it transcended
all other birds.

This was a day when all seemed serene
and the sky blue, with puffy shaped clouds
being carried hurriedly on their way
by the gentle breeze that blew.
My heart leapt as a deer startled by my presence,
ran through the nearby trees to take cover.
A small rabbit sat close, a very young one,
who knew not fear, and all flowers
of assorted colours grew around,
and in the tall blades of grass –
what a beautiful sight –
enough to open wide the heart of any being –
to say

thank you Divine Spirit.

Om.

Preparation for Pure Meditation

'A Crown Jewel'

Pure Meditation is a means of finding one's true self. Being in harmony with life, everyone and every thing. It is a necessity for this day and age because there is so much stress, and so many people are unable to find peace within themselves – because of this fact alone, people will suffer physically as well as mentally and spiritually.

This has nothing to do with religion, it is a truth and a fact, yet with Pure Meditation *all this* can be changed. Dearest Ones, true Meditation, Pure Meditation is learning to concentrate on the Divine power (God) within ourselves, truly this is so. We are part of a whole (part of God) our problem is, that we forget this simple *fact*.

Firstly you must learn to sit very quietly for a few minutes each day, preferably before the day starts and just before bedtime. Use either the word *PEACE* or *LOVE* while you are sitting for your few moments, – as you breathe in, think of the word, as you breathe out, think of the word again and see it cascading through your whole body.

Keep your mind on the word not the breath.

Stay concentrated with thought on these words as you let your breath come and go, then when you feel it's time to finish in the stillness… ask that the day may be as it should and that life's DIVINE WILL be done.

Already you will have set the right course for the day – now go with the day. Live each moment truly as though it is your last; working well, loving and caring for others and of course yourself. If you cannot love yourself or others then try to understand and *like* them.

If during the day you feel tense or out of harmony with life, use the Divine PEACE or LOVE breath again.

At the end of the day, sit, give thanks for EVERYTHING that has happened, Yes – I do mean the problems as well as the happy moments, for this allows conscious thought of the fact that we do progress from our problems and trials… happy times are our holiday… *time off.*

Another principle is to reflect on ourselves once or twice a week, after sitting quietly, to see if we could have done better during the week. Get rid of any *thought rubbish* in a mental dustbin (put the lid back on) and resolve to try better the next day, or the next time we have an opportunity.

How about a mental 'shower' to cleanse all of you after a busy day? always useful. Sit, take in breath and mentally turn on a tap above your head. As it turns, and you breathe out, you mentally visualise and feel a shower of cleansing energy pouring over and around you. See it as *you wish*. But do remember to turn the tap off when you feel sufficiently cleansed, because we are dealing with energies.

Whenever you use any of these spiritual and scientific formulas, do finish by giving thanks and encircling yourself in a white light.

These are some principles that will prepare you for Pure Meditation and also help you at the same time. When you feel ready for a further step along the path of Meditation and really inwardly desire it, then ask that you may find the teacher or guide (Guru) for you. It is a true saying

Ask and you shall Receive

Knock and the door is Opened.

There was a man who loved God

His voice sang his praises and
his tales told were beautiful
Upon waking he would say ' God love me'.
When sleep descended he would cry, 'Love me
God'.
Until one day he was near to the end
of his life span…

He heard a voice from afar saying,
'I have ALWAYS LOVED you my child'.

AUM

ALL the subjects and things I write of here
I have, over the years experienced and found
to be… *TRUTH.*

I would not wish people to have 'blind' faith
in that, which I write of here, for blind faith is
non–progressive and stagnant.

But I do ask, for the reader not to waste their time,
by reading and not using the contents as
'food for thought'.
My only reason for this book is for the truth
to be known.

FOR KNOWLEDGE SHALL SET US FREE.

Questions on Meditation

Many people are interested in Meditation, its origin, practice, and effect.

Therefore it is important to incorporate in this book, some of the many questions that have been asked.

I cannot, unfortunately, put them all here, there are too many, and when one Meditates, the questions are forever coming and being asked of myself, and others who guide in Meditation.

This is a very important part in Meditation. To have a teacher and guide available for this purpose, also that those perplexed do not feel out on a 'limb'.

Both before and after the Pure Meditation Course, it is important that all the questions are answered. Hence the reason for

Guru and guide in this most
important, science and
Spiritual knowledge quest
of
Pure Meditation.

Questions Answered

Why should we Meditate?

It is our spiritual food. We need to Meditate to live properly and get the best out of life. Live life to the full in a balanced and harmonious way, helping you to achieve your needs and fulfil your potential.

To Meditate helps us find our pathway back to our true spiritual self – *SELF~REALIZATION* and *GOD~REALIZATION* – To become truly at one with the universal divine energy – *AND KNOW THAT WE ARE GODS.*

Why bother to live?

We live to progress. Find out about ourselves – change ourselves for the better. Without coming to life – to live again, we cannot find the *KINGDOM OF GOD* – which is of perfect peace… perfect love… perfect wisdom.

Surely just working on loving all of life, will achieve the same as Meditation?

Over the many hundreds of your lifetimes – Yes, but why wait that long? While we have ego, we cannot find this unconditional love for everyone, all the time, easily. We need the knowledge of how to put this into practice. Pure Meditation will give us all the knowledge that we need in our life's journey and certainly how to awake the love within us, to do this 'not so easy task' of loving all of life, sharing it and giving to all as we wisely need to.

Most Meditation practices seem to be linked to belief in a God. What if you do not believe, can you still Meditate and would it benefit you?

Non-belief in a God, does not necessarily mean no belief in a higher power. Disbelief likewise, does not mean they *do* not exist. Most people have some belief that there is some intelligence behind creation. Pure Meditation puts you *in* touch with that intelligence.

If you do not believe – Pure Meditation will change your disbelief to belief by direct contact with your Higher Self (God or *The* Intelligence). It does not matter what we call it. Are we not all unbelievers until we have knowledge to know and believe?… yes! you can still Meditate.

The benefit of Pure Meditation is that it will bring such helpful changes into our life, that we really cannot afford to go through our life without it.

The word scientific as applied to Pure Meditation seems to me dry and unloving?

The root of the word 'science' is 'to know'. In Pure Meditation we seek to 'know about ourselves', life and God into a real down-to-earth way.

There is nothing abstract about Pure Meditation. It is about being wiser and more loving. Yes a 'science' but based much more on fact than theory.

How long should I Meditate for?

It is quality not quantity that counts.

You need to stay for at least half an hour twice a day to begin with, to give yourself time to settle the body, and adjust your thinking pattern… then Meditate. One hour is best suited. The longer you Meditate with desire and concentration, the quicker you get to your *goal*. It is important that you build your Pure Meditation to be of longer periods of time. Not shorter, for only by doing this will you reap the fullest benefits.

Why can't you mix Meditation practices, if you take the best from all of them?

If you do not Meditate then you would not know what *is* the best from all.

A perfect Meditation incorporates *the best* of all – with nothing lacking. It also can only be taught, properly, to you under the guidance of a highly advanced soul, who can see and feed your needs by their wisdom and intuitiveness.

Too many mixes – Spoil
Intellect thinks it knows best.

♦

I only have time to Meditate now and again, is this okay?

Some Meditation is better than none. Though we should not be 'fair weather' people with any given situation. So why with your Meditation? God is your friend, your creator. What if God said 'I only have *time* to be with you and help you now and again – when there is time!' What would you think and feel?

We have time for everything, anything that we *want* to do. The important issue is – how much do you want to Meditate?

The Infinite gives us time in the day to Meditate... if only for a short while. If we do not find the time, in all probability we are bad organisers, or have put too many lesser things in front of the most important one, *PURE MEDITATION*.

♦

Can I pass on what I learn to others?

It is best not to. It is only our ego, that makes us want to tell others and you will not, perhaps, remember clearly enough, to see the pitfalls that are there, awaiting you by doing so.

It is a Jewel, guard it as such while you practise. Remember, others can do harm to you and your Pure Meditation by their thoughts and speech as you can in turn do harm to others.

Guide them to someone who will teach them everything *properly*. Then you will not incur karma, and will know *all* will be well.

I'm a little put out by the idea that you should not have sex before or after Meditation.

Making love to your partner in a loving, caring and giving way can obviously be a great enhancement to your relationship, there is nothing wrong with that. However, we must be aware, that we, like the rest of life, are made up of energy, and are affected to a lesser or greater degree by the interplay of energies. In Meditation we are trying to calm the physical and mental energies, in order to become in tune with higher spiritual energies. Sexual acts stimulate, then scatter the energies, making it harder work to calm our energies for Meditation. It is best not to mix them for this reason alone, otherwise experience will show you it is unadvisable.

Certainly love-making is enhanced by Pure Meditation, when kept separate, for the simple reason that Pure Meditation enhances your general awareness and sensitivity, and your ability to give and receive love on and at all levels.

How do you stop your concentration from wandering?

Most minds do wander 'til you master them. You do this by learning to put a hundred percent concentration into everything that you do – however small it may be. Secondly, when you do find your mind wandering, bring it back gently and lovingly to the thought in mind. Be patient with yourself, in the knowledge that we all have to learn the *art* of concentration. We are bereft of much in life without this ability.

Should one abstain from sex altogether or partially?

Do not over-indulge is the answer here. If a couple are advanced enough, and wish not to have this active part of their relationship, that's fine. If people still feel the need for a sexual relationship, then it would be wrong... and would only do them harm to give it up completely at that time. It was given for procreation. Nowadays, it is treated as a must for our manhood and womanhood. How wrong that is; loving each other can be beautiful. Do keep the balance.

How can I tell when I'm progressing in my Meditation?

We know by our feelings, which will become more peaceful, we feel more at one with life. We try to understand people around us more, and criticise less. Our family and friends are the first to notice this change in us. When this change comes about, do not try to analyse it, but be grateful for the change and spend more time Meditating.

Is there any time when I should not Meditate?

Yes there are times. Leave a gap of at least two to three hours after a meal, and half an hour before a meal, depending on its size. Not immediately after making love with your partner. Not after drinking alcohol; while the alcohol is still with you. When we have acute spinal trouble or towards the latter end of pregnancy. A meditative state would be acceptable here, but not Meditation.

♦

How can I tell when it is progressive to sit for a longer period of time?

It is always worthwhile sitting for a longer period of time – *particularly* when you do **not** feel like doing so. We should make our Meditation longer – never shorter. We Meditate for our own progress, so when we find the peace through our Meditation, we should stay to experience the Bliss that one day we shall find. Always stay 'til you find the peace – even if it seems impossible – Stay – find *your* peace – for without peace we, and others, suffer.

♦

Am I failing if I have a bad Meditation?

The answer is no, you are not failing. Surely by the very fact you are sitting there means you are *trying*. Every time we sit in Meditation it is different, some-times it is better than other times. But being different, means we never are bored, for we never know what is going to happen. It is an adventure, joyous, beautiful and very progressive for us.

Do your best, remember – from any Meditation, the fact of you going and sitting, if nothing else, will bring you progress, but to find Self–Realization, we must apply ourselves with determination and patience – never looking for the end result. Just go into Meditation as you would go to see your *VERY BEST FRIEND*.

I feel others find a state of bliss more quickly. Why?

How do you know? You are only assuming. We must all travel the same path and experience the same difficulties. Some people may be more desirous than others, which will help their progress as it would in any learning capacity. There are souls that would have Meditated in a past life, and therefore will find it easier in this lifetime, which is another good reason for Meditation *NOW*. Do not look for *states* in other people or for yourself. Concern yourself *only* with *yourself* and *your progress*.

Is it more helpful to Meditate with other people, or alone?

To begin with it is far better to Meditate with others, in a group, providing they are all Meditating, for then, the *LIGHT* produced from just one soul who is Meditating will help others who are finding difficulty, – of course it is wise to Meditate on your own as well. It is usually self–consciousness that makes us feel unable to Meditate with others around us.

We should by rights have our eyes closed, and be concentrating *only* on what we are doing. Persevere.

How can I explain my Pure Meditation to others when they ask?

Do not try to, particularly while you find difficulty. It is your own private *'JEWEL'*. Keep it lest it gets torn from you by dissection and criticism. Pure Meditation is difficult to explain to others. Send them to someone who knows how to do this – this is a true chance to help them on to a better path. It's ego that makes people want to explain – to show they know – and air their knowledge. Don't do it.

What should I do when people make fun of my Meditation?

How can they – if you do not talk about it, or try to air your knowledge? Even if they do – it is best to be calm, kind and say nothing.

You do not have to 'stick up' for Meditation, it (like God) can stand up for itself.

How can I stop the body complaining and intruding on my Meditation?

By staying with your Meditation, until it stops. Do some Hatha Yoga, or simple stretching exercise before you start Meditating. Then get yourself in a devotional state in whatever way suits you. Now sit and Meditate, and you will find your body will respond... with peace.

The body is not used to sitting for Meditation. It is used to being told, lying down means sleep, sitting – meals, television or talk; so have patience with your body. Talk to it – tell it what you are doing and what it has to do.

Does it matter having noise in the area when Meditating?

No, it is very good to learn to Meditate with noise. Once you have learnt the art of this, you can Meditate anywhere; though to learn this way may be more difficult to begin with.

Do you have to Meditate to give healing?

No, but healing is only as good as the healer. So I would say learn to Meditate before you start healing.

By working in this way, the patient will receive much more benefit, and you will not only receive benefit as well, but will be a much wiser, and more caring person, when you do give a healing.

I sit and do visualisations, is that Pure Meditation?

Visualisation is nothing like Pure Meditation. It is a method used whereby we bring extra power to our thought by visualising the happenings we want to take place, e.g. in cancer, it is seeing the unwanted cells as being swept away or destroyed, and the body's natural balance and health being restored.

Visualisation is programming the mind. If we use it in a positive way we can change our mood, e.g. from despair to happiness, release inner resentment, and enjoy the relaxation of the feelings brought by our favourite colours, people and places.

Pure Meditation goes far beyond programming of the mind to what really is – to who we really are – expanding our consciousness further than the limitations of our minds.

I have heard that Meditation will make you weak, if practised by a Westerner because our bodies are not suited to this?

This is not so, our bodies are made to adapt to different chemical changes; change of food, thought for example, so therefore, our bodies will accept Meditation.

It is not what you do, so much as *how* you do… what you do. More than this – our bodies *need* Meditation.

Is Pure Meditation dangerous if you are living a busy lifestyle?

Once you have put Pure Meditation *into* your life, it will help you *in* your busy lifestyle, by enabling you to do just as much if not more, without rushing around wasting precious energy; or, worrying whether you can achieve everything that you set out to do that day. It's a must for you.

Can people be damaged by Meditation?

Only if you go to someone who has set themselves up as a teacher of Meditation. It is bestowed on an individual to guide people in Meditation, when that person is wise and can love unconditionally – they are egoless beings. Less than this, yes it could do harm because of the ego *within* the student as well as within the teacher.

What is Pure Meditation and what is Meditative State?

A Meditative State calms the breath and the mind, being beneficial for all who have not yet learned to Meditate, and for times when Meditators are unable to practice their Meditation, for example during illness.

Many people think they are practising Meditation when they go into a Meditative State but the difference is greater than between taking one step up a mountain and travelling to the top.

Pure Meditation is a far deeper state, bringing the peace and bliss of oneness. It is beyond definition, ever new, ever joyful and leads to Self~Realization. If our 'Meditation' does not give us everything we need for progress in life, then it is probably, in truth, a Meditative State or perhaps not a Meditation that feeds us at all our different levels of Being.

Do we have to be celibate to become Self~Realized?

No, you do not need to be celibate, but be balanced in any *activity*. Lahiri Mahasaya, a great Indian Sage had a wife, was a householder. He was Self–Realized. This Pure Meditation is for all peoples, of all religions and all races. Whether they be celibate, householder, homo/heterosexual.

God loves you all and knows how Pure Meditation can give you *EVERYTHING THAT YOU NEED IN TIME.*

What benefits do you get from Pure Meditation?

One should not go into Meditation for any benefits, only to give back love and devotion to *OUR* Infinite Beloved Creator. Having said this the benefits are many, one being that you are helped through your whole life.

Find Self~Realization through Pure Meditation and you will look back for nothing. For God helps those ~ who help themselves.

I have heard that some people get rich by Meditating on making money?

There is a given method by which people mistakenly, try to do this. Money can provide us with mortal comforts but it does not necessarily make us happy. I would say these people are courting danger – far better to ask that their needs be met.

Have we not read about, or seen on television, people who have won thousands, or millions, of pounds and live to regret it slowly.

If we are to have money – God knows – we will.

As soon as I try to go into the stillness, my mind is bombarded by thoughts. Why, and what can I do about it?

This is a perfectly normal thing to happen. Our minds and thoughts are not used to being mastered. They do not like being told what to do. We must understand this. Each time our thoughts stray, we can mentally bring them back; keep doing this, and little by little, they will cease their wanderings, providing you keep them strictly and lovingly under the control of your mind.

Practise and patience will make for perfection.

Sometimes my heart begins to beat furiously and I experience extreme panic. What is happening?

This will usually happen after we have stilled our five senses to a degree, and then we allow an unwanted thought to enter, which sets our five senses, particularly our heart (which starts pounding) into motion again.

Throw out the unwanted thought, and start *stilling* your senses all over again, whilst affirming to your mind, that you will not let your mind wander again.

I like to Meditate at the start of the day, but with a family it's impossible. Please can you help me?

I understand what you are saying. But *nothing* is impossible – there is no such word. Reorganise yourself. Get up earlier or get the children to sit with you. Failing that, Meditate later on in the morning and when they have gone to bed at night. Tell your partner that you need this time to find the peace. If you haven't got a special room, do not be afraid of Meditating while your partner is reading a book.

It is amazing how people and conditions change for us – if we are sincere with our desires.

Is it wrong to fall asleep while Meditating?

There is no wrong or right. If you are very tired and have not exercised, you may fall asleep for a short while. Try not to let it become a habit. Real Meditation is about being in a very wakeful state. Try to Meditate before you get too tired, or rest, and then Meditate.

Be understanding, but *firm* with the resolution not to let it happen. It shows a lack of concentration and love when it happens.

Can I Meditate in bed?

Bed is not the ideal place for Meditation.

The body wants to sleep, making Meditation very hard for you. If there is no other way because of *in extremis*, then and only then, do so, in the knowledge that to Meditate in bed is better than no Meditation.

My partner is suspicious of meditation and resentful of my interest. How can I pursue my spiritual path without antagonism and constant interruptions?

Go about your Meditation very quietly; preferably, Meditate when they are not there, at least, for the moment. I believe, in time, as he/she sees the wonderful change in you taking place, they could well start asking questions. Be careful, you answer simply and without any desire to change them, otherwise it will scare them away again.

Change can only come about in this way, and not by 'bullying' or criticism. Do not feel – or look hard done by – as really you are fortunate to have the knowledge of Pure Meditation, whereas, your partner has not got this knowledge yet.

I have been married three times. Do we have to meet all our partners when we pass?

No, we only meet those we want to. Our love and desire to meet them brings them into our orbit. If we do not love them – they will not come. So it is really up to you!

Do we have to be saints to be Self–Realized, or lose our zest for living?

No, of course not, the only difference between a Saint and a sinner is that 'Saints never give up trying'. What is a Saint? If it is someone who by being wise, thoughtful and loving is given the power to change life and people, then that person would have more zest for life.

In fact, they would have more of everything good, that he or she is, and was, before their Self-Realization came into being.

BE YOUR TRUE SELF AND PUT GOD
INTO YOUR LIFE — LOVE ALL.

♦

Will Pure Meditation help with my relationships?

Decidedly so, Pure Meditation helps us see more clearly our loved ones. It not only gives us clarity of ourselves and others, but allows us to be forgiving, caring and loving in the process. And they in turn make a change for the better, quite often without realization of this fact.

♦

I like some ritual before Meditation, is this acceptable?

Yes it is acceptable, and as long as you feel the need of rituals, you should incorporate them — but not so many as to take your mind off the true purpose of Meditating.

Music, candles and chants all have their place before Meditation. It is important to remember that only when we are in the silence —

do we hear the higher intuitive voice within.

Can I get to God without a Guru?

It is very hard to get to God without a 'dispeller of darkness', over hundreds and thousands of years you can.

We must all get back to God someday.

Having a Guru makes the difference between walking and flying to God. You would not try to learn how to fly without some helpful tuition, so with Meditation. Get help.

Can we take a backward step, ever, in this life, if we Meditate. With problems I mean?

No, if we Meditate properly, it is impossible to do so. Meditation keeps us forever going forward and our problems, if taken as useful experiences, only help us all the more on our forward path.

Can anyone, in any religion learn how to Meditate?

Meditation can be enjoyed by anyone in any religion, for in the very sense of the word, it is a way of life. A path to reap the best *in* life, with *no* dogma, only truth, truth, and more Truth.

How do I know there is a Higher Power?

How do you know *you* are *you?* You don't know, you just feel it. We have to learn with knowledge which leads to firm belief.

For we live by it.

*If you have any further questions,
please ask your tutor on
the Pure Meditation Course.*

◆

Without Pure Meditation
you have to break bad habits by yourself
With Pure Meditation
you **are helped** to break them
by slowly
dissolving them

◆

Aspects of God

An Angel

An Angel is one who cares, who watches, waits and prays for all. They are of love, of kindness and compassion. There to An~gel for us.

Door Keepers

We have a Door Keeper – keeping an eye open for us. Helping us to keep to our pathway. They try to *prevent harm* happening to us unless karmically it must.

If you have ever been pushed out of the way of a car, or prevented from a bad accident. Think and thank your personal Door Keeper.

Gurus

Gurus come in all guises.

They have a body and name, but, are neither, nor are they of gender.

Within they are pure spirit, given a body and personality.

They have no need ~ for they have OM.

They are born to help, teach God's truths. Love all of God's creatures.

Be servant to all yet subservient to none. Only God rules their heart and soul. Their wisdom is deep – passeth all understanding except to those of like mind

Be wise and heed them. Do not take their name in vain for the Father is protective of them.

God

God IS – always has BEEN – EVER WILL BE.

Omnipresent. Unknown yet also can be known.

God is within ALL of life, not one single *thing* is without God's energy.

God is within each and every one, so we are Gods in the MAKING.

God is the purest of LIGHTS.

God's gifts to his children are the CHRIST POWER, Holy Spirit and FREE WILL.

God is truth, compassion, love, understanding, all that is good – perfect in all dimensions of THE LIGHT.

God LOVES unconditionally with no criticism or judgement.

We CAN know God and become more God-like by keeping his commandments. By 'doing unto others as you would be done by'.

One day we shall be ONE with God – Be Gods.

Meditate – keep faith – and as you progress towards Self-Realization so you will unfold THE GOD within.

Man and Woman

Man and woman are in the world to be helpmates to each other. To help each other so that the path of life becomes easier. They also are given the role of propagation. The roles given to them are numerous, though the most purposeful role is that of helping each other to Self~Realization, finding THE GOD within. For, each is a separate SOUL and should not mistake the purpose for which God has made a man and woman. If they forget this fundamental factor and start relying on and giving more devotion to their partner than to God, then the partnership or marriage will never reach its fruition.

The man must find and balance his female energy with his male energy and likewise the woman must find her male energy and balance that energy with her female one, thus, one becomes completely balanced in their 'Yin and Yang' bringing within it peace and harmony. Not only are we on this earth plane to do this but also to change our ego/pride energy into humble selfless loving energy. So we work our way back to the once God~like state that existed within, before our fall from grace.

*Sex **may seem** the greatest*
*God **is** the greatest*

'Sail' through your life

Visualise – you are a beautiful ship… sailing, on course, through life. We must be *master* of our ship (mind and body); to know when to set the sails full mast, to go faster, or to lower them enabling us to go at a slower pace.

We may be tossed by the sea of our *feelings* and *emotions,* or, have a gentle breeze with the sun shining, giving us our *peaceful times.*

Either way we must sail backwards or forwards; which way, depends on how we face up to our life, our problems, and how we deal with them!

Our ship will sail well for us, if we are in command, at the helm.

Be the master of your ship at all times, so that you navigate a straight and good path through the sea of life.

You will never be happy if you travel in the wrong directions or have to 'tack' to get back on your rightful path again.

Man the ship
Calm the seas
Be master of all you survey

Five Stages of Mental Relaxation

1 Most people go through life restless. They cannot close their eyes and hold the eyeballs still, keep the body motionless, or concentrate on one thing at a time; yet peace and calm concentration are in our souls and of its true nature. This being restless all the time without being restful is the first stage.

✹

2 By practice of Pure Meditation, the person who is always mentally restless succeeds in becoming, once in a while, restful, though still restless most of the time. This is the next stage.

✹

3 By further practice this person can develop a calmness to a point where he is able to attain restfulness fairly easily, but can easily be made restless by environment or events.

✹

4 With deeper practice of concentration, Pure Meditation, and by Higher lessons learnt from a true Guru/

Master, the student will then find himself restful most of the time, and restless only occasionally. So we see it is possible by scientific Meditation to reverse one's untrue nature.

✦

5   With continual practice of Pure Meditation methods given by a true Guru who must be a God Realized person, the student will reach the fifth stage in Meditation, Samadhi, whereby the devotee feels he and God are as one. It is completely the reverse of the first stage, and can only be obtained by being able to enter *SAMADHI* at will, any time, any where.

✦

For You

When you feel alone,
remember me.

When your heart is heavy with sorrow.
Think of me.

And when you long for peace,
feel my hand upon your brow.

Do not forget
I am with you always.

Wonderment

This Chapter is finally to put the viewpoint that only love – Unconditional Love will bring us our freedom. If we would, but, remember, two lines ~

Love everyone and everything as seen to be yourself.

Do unto others as you would be done to.

Surely with following, always, these two golden rules of life, we would be doing the very best that we could, and this in turn, would make our pathway to wonderment and joy.

Love is God

Light is God

All is God

We Are

The wonderment is why, we cannot see these simple facts and principles of life that are spiritually uplifting, yet, so sensible and 'down to earth'.

Learn to have Faith

Learn to Love

Do your Best

and that is all that is ever truly asked of us.

my dear souls,

  we are all ONE
  let us love as one
  and live as ONE

    So

peace may reign on this
earth plane and the whole
  universe.

    I

leave you now and
always with my
unconditional Love
and blessings to you
  all.

Mata yogananda

Beliefs and Aims of the Centre

1. The spreading of the truth.

2. That there is no death, only organised life.

3. That scientific and spiritual knowledge lead to Self–Realization, peace and harmony.

4. To bring harmony to the mind, body and spirit of all living creatures.

5. To show that *LOVE* is the strongest energy force that there is, anywhere.

6. To show that all people and all religions will lead eventually to the one and same pathway, to Self~Realization and God~Realization.

7. That knowledge will dispel ignorance and fear and make us whole.

8. To provide pure thoughts to beget high minds.

9. To find our true selves through Pure Meditation.

10. To show how to rid ourselves of all negative states of the mind and body.

11. To spread unconditional love throughout the world.

12. To uphold the wisdom of the Masters, such as Ji Jesus, Babaji, Buddha and the Saints.

13. To prove that there are many Masters and many Mansions – for us all.

For information on **Pure Meditation**, Retreats, Progressive Counselling, Natural Spiritual Healing, Transformation Hatha Yoga and other Courses, please contact us at:

Self Realization Meditation Healing Centre

Laurel Lane, Queen Camel, Yeovil,
Somerset, BA22 7NU, UK.
Tel. 01 935 850266   Fax. 01 935 850234

email: info@selfrealizationcentres.org
Internet: http:\\www.selfrealizationcentres.org
UK Registered Charity No. 800412

Sister Centres

18 Cunliffe Place, Glenfield, Auckland,
New Zealand. Ph./Fax. 09 441 9446

100 Highsted Road, Bishopdale,
Christchurch, **New Zealand**.
Ph. 03 359 8507   Fax. 03 359 3430

8904 Armstrong Way, Halfmoon Bay,
B.C., VON 1Y2, **Canada**.
Tel. & Fax. (604) 740 0898

7187 Drumheller Road, Bath,
Michigan, 48808, **USA**
Ph. (517) 641–6201Fax. (517) 641 8336

Edwinsford, Talley, Llandeilo,
Carmarthenshire, **Wales** SA19 7BX
Tel. 01558 685565 Fax. 01558 685871

Contact Centres:

Australia, Blue Mountains:
Tel/Fax. 02 4756 2042
Mobile 0415 543473

Switzerland, Langenthal:
Tel. 062 922 8187   Fax. 062 922 8127

Contacts in:

Carterton, New Zealand
London and Brighton, England
Edinburgh, Scotland
For other areas and details please enquire.

Light Up The World!

Meditation Evenings Worldwide ~ to bring souls together to imbibe and go forward to Self–Realization.

It was with great joy that the first Open Meditation Evening was held at the Mother Centre many years ago; souls coming together to imbibe Divine Peace and Love, to seek Self–Realization through Pure Meditation. Since that time many Open Meditation Evenings have come into being around the world ~ like stars of Love shining their light into the darkness of separation, delusion and suffering.

We hope that many more souls will be moved to open their hearts and their homes in this way, until the world is full of the Light it so urgently needs.

We look forward to you joining us ~ in the list that follows you will find your nearest SRMHC Meditation Evening. Please ring for details.

These Meditation Evenings and the Arms of the Family, are expanding all the time ~ please contact the UK Mother Centre for further details and contacts.

The peace~oneness in Meditation ~ joy for all to share.

✪ UK Mother Centre
Somerset, Queen Camel ◆ Monday - Saturday 8.45 for 9pm Meditation, Sundays 7.45 for 8pm Meditation (01935) 850266

✪ *UK*

Bath ✦ first Tuesday of each month, 8pm Meditation
Jill Lambert ✦ (01225) 312233

Bristol, Lower Knowle ✦ Thursdays weekly 8.30pm ✦ Paul
and Sheran Beard ✦ (0117) 977 0800

Bristol, Pensford ✦ Mondays 8.30pm weekly ✦ Julia Raffo
(01761) 490556

Bristol, St. Andrews ✦ 8.30pm last Tuesday of each month
Lindy Gibbon ✦ (0117) 944 2711

Devon, Newton Abbott ✦ 7.45pm for 8pm Meditation, first
Sunday of each month ✦ Rowena Dharma Nicholson and
Jason Hinrich ✦ (01803 872041)

Devon, South Molton ✦ 6.30 for 7pm Meditation, first
Thursday of each month ✦ Sarah Beanland ✦ (01769) 540080

Dorset, Poole ✦ 7.45 for 8pm Meditation, first Thursday of
each month ✦ Marie Fraser Nash ✦ (01202) 699313

London, N19 ✦ from 6pm, first Sunday of each month
Deborah Munnelly ✦ (0207) 700 6557

Scotland, Edinburgh ✦ Sunday afternoons weekly, 3.15 for
3.30pm Meditation ✦ Satay Singh ✦ (0131) 467 0828/
Mobile 07708 796 737

Somerset, Chewton Mendip ✦ Thursdays weekly 8.50pm
Janet North ✦ (01761) 241650

Somerset, Frome ✦ Wednesdays 8.30pm weekly and other
times by request ✦ Charles Kemp and Sara Crowley
(01373) 462606

Somerset, Glastonbury ✦ Wednesdays, weekly 7.45 for 8pm
Meditation ✦ Carol and Terry Palmer ✦ (01458) 831353

Somerset, Martock ✦ Tuesdays weekly, 8.45 for 9pm
Meditation ✦ Rossananda and Mahseeman Seva Young
(01935) 824142

Somerset, Wells ✦ Tuesdays weekly, 7.45 for 8pm
Meditation ✦ Joy Buchanan ✦ (01934) 712082 ✦ Caroline
Bruce ✦ (01749) 870873

Surrey, Farnham ✦ Tuesdays weekly, 7.45 for 8pm
Meditation ✦ Monica Walton ✦ (01252) 734659
Sussex, Brighton ✦ Wednesdays weekly 8.15 for 8.30pm
Fiona Williams ✦ (01273) 550645
Wales, Llandeilo ✦ Monday - Saturday 8.45 for 9pm
Meditation, Sundays 7.45 for 8pm Meditation ✦ Wales
SRMH Centre ✦ (01558) 685565
Yorkshire, Richmond ✦ 8.30pm first Wednesday of each
month ✦ Maureen Clayton ✦ (01748) 886188

✪ *Australia*

Blue Mountains, Mount Wilson, ✦ Sundays 7.30pm
weekly ✦ Suzzane and Denis Daly ✦ 024756 2042/Mobile
0415 543473

✪ *Canada*

British Columbia, Halfmoon Bay ✦ Monday-Saturday 8.45
for 9pm Meditation, Sundays 7.45 for 8pm Meditation
Canadian SRMH Centre ✦ (604) 740 0898
British Columbia, North Vancouver ✦ 10.30am, third
Sunday of each month Noel Hanuse ✦ (604) 983 9661

✪ *Germany*

Baden-Wuerttemberg, Waldkirch ✦ 9am, first Sunday of
each month ✦ Renate Scholz Suchant ✦ 07681 490329

✪ *Ireland*

Dublin, Dun Laoghaire ✦ Monday and Thursday evenings
weekly 8.15 for 8.30pm Meditation ✦ Bernadette
McPhillips ✦ 00353 1214 5964/Mobile 00353 87 132 8579

✪ *New Zealand*

South Island, Christchurch ✦ Monday-Saturday 8.45 for
9pm Meditation, Sundays 7.45 for 8pm Meditation
Christchurch SRMH Centre ✦ (03) 359 8507
North Island, Auckland ✦ Sundays 7.45 for 8pm Medita-
tion, Mondays and Thursdays 8.45 for 9pm Meditation
Auckland SRMH Centre ✦ (09) 441 9446

South Island, Dunedin ✦ 7.45pm first Wednesday of each month and at other times by request ✦ Jan Stenhouse (03) 455 4463

North Island, Warkworth (Matakana) ✦ Sundays 7.45 for 8pm first & third Sunday of each month
Colette Taylor ✦ (09) 422 5255

North Island, Masterton ✦ Sundays 7.45 for 8pm Meditation
Ràna Webster and Dev Verma ✦ (06) 379 7459

✪ *Switzerland*

Switzerland, Brig-Glis ✦ Wednesdays 8pm twice monthly
Franziska Fischer ✦ 062 922 8187

Switzerland, Hinwil ✦ 9.30am second Sunday of each month ✦ Anita Wick ✦ 01 937 4204

Switzerland, Langenthal ✦ Tuesdays 8.45pm weekly
Franziska Fischer ✦ 062 922 8187

Switzerland, Trin ✦ Thursdays 8.30pm weekly
Lisbeth Gilgen ✦ 081 6 35 1592

✪ *USA*

Michigan, Lansing ✦ Monday - Saturday 8.45 for 9pm Meditation, Sundays 7.45 for 8pm Meditation, Michigan SRMH Centre ✦ (517) 641 6201

The Arms of the Family offer bed and breakfast and/or dinner to students/friends of the worldwide Self Realization Meditation Healing Centres: for those friends who are travelling and wish to find a loving place to rest their heads 'en route' and know that they will be welcome. In this way we hope to bring a sharing of life with those of a like mind.

Please ring the UK Mother Centre for further contacts and details.

♥ UK

Bristol, Nailsea ♦ Roger Furneaux ♦ (01278) 751493

Bristol, Pensford ♦ Julia Raffo♦ (01761) 490556

Dorset, Drimpton ♦ Alison Hunt ♦ (01308) 867071/Mobile 07775 862776

Somerset, Martock ♦ Rossananda and Mahseeman Seva Young (01935) 824142

Somerset, Wells ♦ Joy and Alan Buchanan ♦ (01934) 712082

Somerset, Wyke Champflower (Nr. Bruton)
Noreen Daniel and Eileen Lemon ♦ (01749) 812788

Wales, Brecon ♦ Gabelle and Michael Eisele
(01874) 690116

Wales, Powys ♦ Mark Chappell ♦ (01686) 412307

Yorkshire, Richmond ♦ Maureen Clayton ♦ (01748) 886188

♥ Australia

Blue Mountains, Mount Wilson ♦ Suzzane and Denis Daly 024756 2042/Mobile 0415 543473

New South Wales, Sydney ♦ Daodeva Westward 02 9896 6917

♥ Canada

Alberta, Edmonton ♦ Keith and Nicole Bradford
(780) 450 9836/Mobile (780) 920 2495

♥ New Zealand

North Island, Masterton ♦ Ràna Webster and Dev Verma (06) 379 7459

♥ Switzerland

Langenthal ♦ Franziska Fischer ♦ 062 922 8187

Trin ♦ Lisbeth Gilgen ♦ 081 635 1592

All the Self Realization Meditation Healing Centres are here for you. If you need further information of any kind, please do contact us.

Other Publications by Mata Yogananda
available from Daoseva Press

Books

THE TRUTH ETERNAL ISBN 0 9522734 4 6
COME~ A Spiritual Journey
ISBN 0 9522734 6 2
POEMS OF THE HEART ISBN 0 9522734 9 7
SONG~SOUL CHANTS Music book
ISBN 0 9522734 3 8
SONG~SOUL CHANTS ("Small songbook")
PERFECT THOUGHTS Music book
SPIRITUAL FAMILIES AND CENTRES ~
an Unknown Journey ISBN 0 9522734 0 3

Videos

Imbibe in Mata Yogananda's wisdom ~ in person.
Centres of Light ★ Talks with Mata Yogananda ★
A Message from Mata ★ Questions and Answers with Mata

Videos are supplied on cassette (VHS/PAL.) Some are available in the VHS/NTSC format. Please contact your nearest Centre for details.

DHARMA *Magazine*

Dharma is the Centres' yearly magazine pre-
senting the Wisdom of God~Life and the
Masters; with articles by Mata Yogananda
and people in different professional fields
including those in holistic health care. The emphasis is
on practical spirituality, covering all aspects of life. Please
contact the Centre to order the current issue of Dharma.
Subscriptions (three and five year) and back issues are
also available. ISSN 1366–3550

Photographs of Mata Yogananda

We are delighted to now have available photographs of Mata Yogananda in a beautiful glossy finish. Yours to treasure, these photos will bring Mata's light to your whole being.

❧

Inspiring Talk Tapes & Song ~ Chants
by Mata Yogananda

In the Inspiring Talks series, Mata Yogananda speaks on real-life issues with **love and understanding**; of the difficulties we all must overcome in our progress back to consciousness of our spiritual nature. Mata has recorded these talks so that her words may reach out to those not able to be with her, but who are needing the encouragement and demonstration that it is possible to live a God–centred life in this world today.

Also available, on CD, are two collections of Mata Yogananda's Song~Chants: *Vibrations of Love* and *Perfect Thoughts*. Each contains Song~Chants given to and performed by Mata Yogananda for the upliftment of all, recorded live, in an informal way in the UK. Companion word and music booklets to each of these beautiful CDs are also available separately.

For all authentic publications of the Self Realization Meditation Healing Centre by Daoseva Press, please contact your nearest authorised dealer or Centre for a full catalogue, prices and availability.

Ten Commandments + 2
for daily consumption

1) To be at all times truthful and honest.

2) practice unconditional love for all of life

3) No judgement or criticism - less you be judged.

4) accept yourself and others at the level they/you are

5) Remember every person is doing their best

6) you are all precious & loved equally by God & Guru.

7) unconditional love conquers all problems

8) The more spiritual wisdom you have — the more humble you must be.

9) always give thanks & say 'thy Will be done'.

10) all service done in love is truly blessed

AS YOU SOW - SO SHALL YE REAP.

11) Do Not let ego or others take you off your path

12) go to God and Guru for your progress and deeper wisdom and understanding

God BLESS you   my

To My Readers

Some may wonder at my using the word God so often in this book, in this day and age.

I use it, for I cannot think of a more beautiful word to describe a higher loving, divine power, of light, unconditional love and pure bliss.

I believe implicitly that we are all part of this higher energy, and that part of us *is perfection,* we have but to unravel ourselves to find it.

We are God